Women's Poems of Protest and Resistance
# Honduras, 2009-2014

*Women's Poems of Protest and Resistance: Honduras, 2009-2014*
Spanish-English Bilingual Edition.
General Editor, Lety Elvir.
Translation Editor, María Roof.
2nd revised, augmented edition and translation of *Honduras: Golpe y pluma, Antología de poesía resistente escrita por mujeres (2009-2013)*. Ed. Lety Elvir. Tegucigalpa: Siguanaba, 2013.
Washington, DC: MACLAS/Casasola LLC/Siguanaba, 2015
© Lety Elvir, this edition
Original poems, © by each poet
Translations, © by each poet
Cover Design and Layout by Casasola Editores.
Cover Picture by Ariel Sosa.
ISBN-10:1942369026
ISBN-13:978-1-942369-02-8

If the translations are used in other publications, in print, online or any other format, please include the name of the translator.
Opinions expressed by the poets and editors are theirs alone and are not subject to approval or comment by the publisher or sponsors.
Casasola LLC ®
***1619 1st St NW, Apt C, Washington, DC 20001***
***Apartado postal 2171, Tegucigalpa, Honduras***

www.casasolaeditores.com

—w—

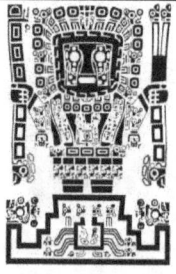 This publication is supported by a grant from the Middle Atlantic Council of Latin American Studies (MACLAS), which is not responsible for the content.
www.maclas.org

Women's Poems of Protest and Resistance
# Honduras, 2009-2014

—ɯ—

Spanish-English Bilingual Edition

—ɯ— —ɯ— —ɯ—

General Editor Lety Elvir

Translation Editor María Roof

CONTENTS

DEDICATION / 10
ACKNOWLEDGEMENTS / 11
EPIGRAPHS / 12
PROLOGUE TO THE BILINGUAL EDITION / 14
ORGANIZATIONS AND ABBREVIATIONS / 19
PRESENTATION OF THE FIRST EDITION / 22
ANTECEDENTS AND JUSTIFICATION / 25
INTRODUCTION: "Poetry Written by Women and the Coup d'État in Honduras, 2009" / 27
Anthology of Women's Poems of Protest and Resistance: Honduras, 2009-2014 / 41
**Soledad Altamirano** / 42
PENA / SHAME
Quedan / What's Left
**Suyapa Antúnez Cerrato** / 46
Abran paso que yo ahí voy / Make Way I'm Coming Through
Delincuentes Uniformados / Crooks in Uniform
Para los que se venden en silencio / For Those Who Silently Sell Out
**Suny del Carmen Arrazola** / 54
(En el futuro...) / (In the Future)
Memoria / Memory
Utopía o muerte / Utopia or Death
**Heidy Barahona Alachán (Heidy Alachán)** / 66
Me dolés país / You Pain Me, Country
Lo invoqué / I Invoked Him
Soy Mujer / I Am Woman
**Gilda Batista** / 72
Ustedes / You People
Solo Quiero Tres / I Just Want Three
AMANECIÓ EN HONDURAS / DAY DAWNED IN HONDURAS
**Rebeca Becerra Lanza** / 80
REFUNDACIÓN / REFOUNDATION
**Noemí Borjas Rodríguez** / 84
Un golpe a la esperanza / A Coup´s Blow to Hope
Bienvenida a un líder / Welcome to a Leader

**Xiomara Bu** / 88
MIEDO / FEAR
Tensión / Tension
MI PATRIA / MY COUNTRY
**Xiomara Cacho Caballero** / 96
Desiguales / Unequals
Licencia para delinquir / License to Commit Crime
Pide a gritos el castigo / Demand Punishment Screaming
**Dora Esperanza Cálix Molina** / 102
Porque me asiste la razón / Because Reason Is on My Side
¿Qué puedes ofrecerme, patria? / What Can You Offer Me, Homeland?
En pocas palabras / In A Few Words
**Doris Melissa Cardoza Calderón** / 110
Plegaria / Prayer
Amar de golpe / To Love All of Sudden
Tengo una hija en la mente / I Have a Daughter in My Mind
**Amanda Castro** / 116
Sirven las palabras... / Words Are Good For...
Que pasen todas las mujeres / Let All the Women Pass
**Yadira Eguigure** / 124
Aquí, en esta Honduras entrañable, se escribe la historia /
  Here, in This Beloved Honduras, History is Written
I. En este país han secuestrado la verdad /
  I. In This Country Truth Has Been Kidnapped
II. Nos recetaron el "aquí no pasa nada" /
  II. They Prescribed to Us the "Nothing Is Happening Here"
**Lety Elvir** / 132
Algunas íes sobre el golpe de estado /
  Dotting Some I's Regarding the Coup
Ustedes / You People
Los muertos en mi país / The Dead in my Country
**Reyna Escobar Trigueros** / 146
HUESOS DE METAL / BONES OF STEEL
**Diana Espinal Meza** / 148
Lázaro se levanta / Lazarus Rises
Se ha quedado varado / It's Ended Up Stranded
Este monosílabo de piedra / This Monosyllable of Stone

[5]

**Indira Flamenco** / 154
Reencuentro / Reencounter
El altar frente al espejo / Altar Facing the Mirror
Salutación a los golpistas / Salutation to the *Golpistas*
**Daysi Flores** / 160
Impotente / Impotent
Imprudente / Imprudent
Leo / Leo
**Armida García Aguilar** / 166
II. Este caldo / II. This broth
XX. Tierra sin puntos cardinales /
    XX. Land without cardinal points
XXI. Aquí / XXI. Here
**Blanca Guifarro** / 172
Caza Blanca en tres actos / White House Hunt in Three Acts
Valle del Aguán / Aguan River Valley
Wendy / Wendy
**Doris Amanda Henríquez** / 182
A mí no me lo contaron / They Didn't Tell Me
**Sofía Alejandra Hernández Motiño** / 184
En mis entrañas te llevo golpe / I Carry You Inside Me, Coup
**Karla Lara** / 186
A Manuel / To Manuel
Recordarles / Remember Them
Cajas de recuerdos / Memory Boxes
**Elisa Logan** / 196
A fuego cruzado / In the Crossfire
Viviendo el evangelio / Living the Gospel
Entre adioses y olvidos y la paz... /
    Between Farewells and Forgetting and Peace...
**Grecia Lozano** / 202
Triste despedida. Hasta luego, Comandante /
    A Sad Goodbye. Farewell, Comandante
El Show del Siglo XXI en Honduras /
    The Show of the 21st Century in Honduras
Libre / Libre-Free
**Waldina Mejía Medina** / 208
Poema para Isy con Honduras / Poem for Isy, for Honduras

**Venus Ixchel Mejía** / 214
¿Dónde está la democracia? / Where is Democracy?
Sin reproche / Without Reproach
Resistencia / Resistance
**Fanny Meléndez** / 224
Otro golpe / Another Blow
Yo soy todas, todos y una /
I Am All Women, All Men, and One
Piensan que se llevarán todo al morir /
They Think They'll Take It All With Them When They Die
**Iris Mencía Bárcenas** / 230
Nada pasa / Nothing's Happening
Tinta y sangre (Elecciones espurias, Honduras 2009) /
Ink and Blood (False Elections, Honduras, 2009)
Estado del tiempo / State of Time
**Melissa Merlo** / 236
El amor es... / Love Is...
Espejo mágico / Magic Mirror
Ignorantia / Ignorantia
**María Tomasa "Tomy" Morales Castillo** / 244
Héroe anónimo / Anonymous Hero
Ni perdón, ni olvido / Neither Forgiving, Nor Forgetting
**Mayra Oyuela** / 248
Cumplir 27 / Turning 27
Nos compromete el grito (o panfleto descarado) /
Our Voice Raised in Protest Obligates Us (or Shameless Rhetoric)
Bajo el tálamo / Under the Marriage Bed
**Stella ("Tita") Pineda Becerra** /256
FILOSOFANDO / PHILOSOPHIZING
LIBERTAD / FREEDOM
**Amada Esperanza Ponce** / 262
Introspección / Introspection
Resonaban como profecías... / They Resounded Like Prophecies
La cárcel / Jail
**Rachel Ramírez** / 268
LAS LOCURAS DE MEL / MEL'S MADNESS

**Déborah Ramos** /276
El canto de Mel y su pueblo en resistencia /
Mel's Song and His People in Resistance
El amor en los tiempos del golpe / Love in the Times of the Coup
El canto de los dioses malos / The Song of the Bad Gods
**Francesca Randazzo** / 286
Soy ese ruido / I Am That Noise
Dónde está el calor / Where Is the Warmth
Tierra que se mueve / Land that Moves
**María Luisa Regalado Morán** /294
A mi niña / To My Girl
**Alfa Reyes** / 306
Sueño para nuestras comunidades /
Dream for Our Communities
**Isabel Rivera** /308
Cuerda floja / Tightrope
El día que mataron a Georgino / The Day Georgino Was Killed
Te conozco / I Know You
**Ela Rosinda Robles Muñoz** / 316
Maestros Combatientes / Combatant Teachers
Audaces Periodistas / Daring Journalists
Xiomara llegó / Xiomara Arrived
**Aleyda Romero** / 322
USTEDES / YOU PEOPLE
**Scarleth I. Romero Cantarero** /324
Hundimiento / Caving In
**Sara Salazar Melendez** / 326
El golpe de estado / Coup d'État
Hondureñas / Honduran Women
Hoy más que nunca / Today More than Ever
**Jéssica Sánchez (Jéssica Isla)**/ 332
Puntos cardinales / Cardinal Points
Rojo / Red
PRESENTACIÓN / PRESENTATION
**Claudia Sánchez Cárcamo** / 342
Valentía / Courage
Raspando ideas / Scraping Ideas
Con que agonía pides que… / With What Agony You Request That…

**Claudia Sosa Elvir** / 352
Arañas y Flores / Spiders and Flowers
Besos y Cuchillos / Kisses and Knives
**Sara Tomé** / 356
Resistencia / Resistance
**Carolina Torres** / 358
¿Qué se hace? / What To Do?
El mal no está en las personas, el mal está en el sistema /
There Are No Bad People, There Is Only a Bad System
10:50 varios días / 10:50 Several Days
**Evelyn Y. Torres Mejía** / 370
Silencio de la noche / Silence of Night
Calles / Streets
Ahora / Now
**Karen Valladares** / 378
Nave de sueños / Ship of Dreams
Ciudad inversa / Inverted City
Ciudad mía / City of Mine
**Diana E. Vallejo** / 384
El pueblo / The People
No hay insultos... ASESINOS... / There Is No Insult... MURDERERS...
Emo (desde Huehuetlapallan) / Emo (from Huehuetlapallan)
**Anarella Vélez Osejo** / 392
Memoria / Memory
Golpes / Coups
Las de hoy / Women Today

APPENDIX: Women's Rights. Excerpt from: "Honduras: Human Rights and the Coup d'État." Report of the Inter-American Commission on Human Rights, Organization of American States, December 30, 2009 / 398

BACK COVER COMENTARY, FIRST EDITION IN SPANISH:
"*Custos, quid de nocte?*" / 405
TRANSLATORS / 406

## DEDICATION

To the women authors of these poems; to the women and men whose struggles, acts of resistance and sacrifices inspired these verses. To my mother and my daughters, for the time I stole from them to devote to this anthology; to my father, for his eternal resistance.

–Lety Elvir

## ACKNOWLEDGEMENTS

Thank you to the poets in this anthology, for your writings, your courage, your acts of resistance, for all you have done and are doing to create a Honduras without undemocratic changes in government, without dictatorships, without violence and without legal impunity.

To Ariel Montes de Oca, poet and friend, for his solidarity and encouragement.

To the marvelous women who helped scour the country for poets and poems written in protest and resistance, especially Zoila Madrid, María Luisa Regalado, Divina Alvarenga, Karla Lara, María Arechaga, Indira Flamenco, Iris Mencía and Melissa Cardoza.

To the talented bilingual translators who generously volunteered their skills and assumed a commitment so that these vital poems could be read by a broader international audience.

Special appreciation to Swiss Cooperation in Latin America, whose valuable contribution and support made possible the publication of the first edition of this anthology.

Our deep appreciation to the Middle Atlantic Council of Latin American Studies (MACLAS) for its support of the publication of this edition.

Our appreciation to Janet N. Gold for permission to cite from her translation of the Clementina Suarez poem "Combat," from *Clementina Suarez: Her Life and Poetry* (Gainesville: University Press of Florida, 1995).

I am a poet
an army of poets.
Today I want to write a poem,
poems that cry out,
poems that are weapons...
Today I want to build and destroy,
raise hope on the scaffolds...
be lightning, thunder...
to raze, to ravage
the rotten roots of my people.

   –Clementina Suárez,
   "Combat"


Honduras is a body that keeps the memory
of resistances by original peoples,
the libertarian mysticism of the Garífuna people,
feminine creativity,
sexual dissidences' ability to challenge,
the courage of insurgent people who face off
                                          against power.
Honduras is a Latin American body that loves,
fights, cares and rebels.
It is a seed that grows in scorched earth.
It is a voice, many voices, that speak the true word.
It is a gigantic bonfire burning lies.
It is a trap set for imperial arrogance...

   –Claudia Korol,
   "Stubborn Tendernesses Drawn on the Skin of Honduras"

"Those who dominate in a certain field are in a position to make it work to their benefit, but they must always consider the resistance, protests, vindications and aspirations, 'political' or not, of the dominated [...] When the dominator manages to crush or dominate the resistance and the reactions of the dominated, the struggle tends to disappear [...] There can be history only as long as individuals rebel, resist and react [...] Dictatorships are an attempt to put an end to history."

–Pierre Bourdieu,
*Responses: Toward A Reflexive Anthropology*

## PROLOGUE TO THE BILINGUAL EDITION

The first edition of this anthology, *Honduras: Golpe y pluma: Antología de poesía resistente escrita por mujeres (2009-2013)*, was researched, compiled, prologued, and edited by poet Lety Elvir in September 2013 in the midst of death threats against several of its authors, unprecedented acts of violence against journalists and other defenders of the constitutionally guaranteed freedom of expression, and rampant attacks on community organizers and farmers claiming land rights, in a seemingly lawless environment of impunity for the perpetrators of certain crimes.

Honduras is touted for touristic purposes by an informational site as "a vibrant country, brimming with clear turquoise waters, pristine beaches, lush jungles, breathtaking mountains, challenging rivers, and fascinating ancient ruins," whose people are known for "the warmth of Honduran hospitality." But a disclaimer appears: "The U.S. State Department notes that the security situation in the country is precarious, due to the country's high crime rate and frequent political demonstrations."[1] Despite bilateral U.S.-Honduras agreements, the State Department recognizes the prevailing level of criminality:

> The vast majority of serious crimes in Honduras, including those against U.S. citizens, are never solved. Members of the Honduran National Police are known to engage in criminal activity, including murder and car theft. The Government of Honduras lacks sufficient resources to properly investigate and prosecute cases, and police often lack vehicles or fuel to respond to calls for assistance. In practice, this means police may take hours to arrive at the scene of a violent crime, or may not respond at all. As a result, criminals operate with a high degree of impunity throughout Honduras. The Honduran government is in the early stages of substantial reforms to its criminal justice institutions.[2]

This situation runs totally counter to the express purpose of United States support for Honduras:

> Our policy in Honduras is focused on strengthening democratic governance, including the promotion of human rights and the

---

[1] Honduras.com. http://www.honduras.com.

[2] U.S. State Department, "Honduras Travel Warning, June 24, 2014." http://travel.state.gov/content/passports/english/alertswarnings/honduras-travel-warning.html.

rule of law, enhancing economic prosperity, and improving the long-term security situation in the country.[3]

Honduras has become the most violent country in Latin America, and, as the U.S. State Department recognizes, "Since 2010, Honduras has had the highest murder rate in the world."[4] This continues to be the official evaluation since one year after the "constitutional crisis" that began on June 28, 2009, with the removal and exile of the elected president, considered a coup d'état by the United States and international entities, including the United Nations, Organization of American States and European Union. Subsequent elections in November 2009 and 2013 brought new elected presidents, but lack of security still creates life-threatening conditions for the Honduran population.

The homicide rate in Honduras is truly astounding and spiked after the 2009 coup, as reported by the United Nations Office on Drugs and Crime:[5]

| YEAR | HOMICIDE RATE PER 100,000 INHABITANTS |
|---|---|
| 2008 | 60.8 |
| 2009 | 70.7 |
| 2010 | 81.8 |
| 2011 | 91.4 |
| 2012 | 90.4 |

The murder rate in Honduras in 2012, the latest year for which data are available, was nearly fifteen times the global average homicide rate of 6.2.[6] This is a clear symptom of an environment of extreme, daily, lived violence. Indeed, as Lety Elvir observed in her prologue to the first edition, "lack of protection from the persistent violation of human rights terrorizes society." Early documentation of sexual violence, physical and verbal abuse, psychological aggression and

---

3 U.S. State Department, Bureau of Western Hemisphere Affairs, Fact Sheet: "U.S. Relations With Honduras," March 24, 2014, http://www.state.gov/r/pa/ei/bgn/1922.htm.
4 "Honduras Travel Warning, June 24, 2014."
5 United Nations Office on Drugs and Crime (UNODC). "2014 Global Study on Homicide. Trends, Contexts, Data," page 126. https://www.unodc.org/documents/gsh/pdfs/2014_GLOBAL_HOMICIDE_BOOK_web.pdf.
6 UNODC. "2014 Global Study," page 12.

death threats gathered by the Inter-American Commission on Human Rights of the Organization of American States is included here in the appendix—the Women's Rights section of the December 30, 2009, report, "Honduras: Human Rights and the *Coup d'Etat*."

In this atmosphere of danger and urgency, the preparation of this bilingual edition was undertaken by a team of twenty volunteer translators, all Latin Americanists well versed in the history and cultures of the region, who translated one or more poets each. Within two weeks of the original call for collaboration to selected colleagues, their commitment was so strong that most had enthusiastically accepted, some had contacted others who also offered their skills, and all the poems had been, or were in the process of being, translated. The translators generously agreed to allow rights to the translations to revert to the poets, with the understanding that use of these translations in any format or media will be attributed to the translator named for that poet. The versions in English were reviewed by the translation editor but generally not by the poets themselves. Biographies of the translators and contact information are included at the end.

Besides its bilingual format, this is a revised and augmented edition. Of the original 47 poets, 46 are included here (one asked to be removed), in addition to 7 new poets, for a total of 53 poets and 131 poems (in contrast to the original 119). A few minor changes were made to the poems in Spanish where errors were noted. Some typographical changes may have occurred to produce a more consistent text. Explanatory notes have been added only where it seemed that a simple online search would not readily yield the relevant information.

ON THE TRANSLATIONS

English has a remarkable ability to adopt foreign words, with common use of Spanish-based "-ista" words such as machista and Sandinista, and the creation of neologisms like barista and fashionista. Since English has no good word for "golpista"—derived from the Spanish "golpe de estado" to name a person who executes or supports a coup d'état, we have kept the term *golpista* here where "overthrowers" seemed less accurate. "Golpe" also commonly means a blow, punch, hit, and its translation here in English depends on the context in which it appears, whereas the word in Spanish simultaneously suggests the action of hitting and a coup.

The poets' plurivalent use of words related to the country's name—"hondo," "hondura," "honduras"—is difficult to suggest in English, which lacks similar Latin-based words related to "deep" or "depth(s)." The origin of the name "Honduras" could lie in the Spanish colonial adaptation of the indigenous "huntulha" referring to a watery coast. But the name is generally attributed to Columbus's 1502 utterance of thanks to God for having left the deep waters off the northern coast during a storm: "Gracias a Dios que hemos salido de estas honduras." Poet Scarleth I. Romero Cantarero's historically resonant "Así me duelen estas honduras," can be properly translated as "This is how these depths pain me," which, however, does not evoke the country's name like the Spanish does. Similarly, Suny del Carmen Arrazola: "en lo hondo / Honduras"—in the depths / deeply Honduran; Amanda Castro: "… el dolor / ése que Hondo nos destrozaba el alma"—the pain / the one that was Deeply destroying our soul; Yadira Eguigure: "En este lugar tan hondo de la América herida"— In this place so deep in wounded America; and Karen Valladares's poetic linkage of Tegucigalpa and "hondura de nostalgia"—depth of nostalgia.

"Nothing is going on; nothing is happening here" was a frequent response from officials, despite sustained, severe repression of acts of resistance, in order to deflect international questions about the post-coup situation in Honduras. Several poets use the phrase ironically, "Aquí no pasa nada," to contrast government cover-up and denials of any cause for alarm against the reality portrayed in their poems.

Unrhymed verses are the norm in contemporary Latin American poetry, but some of the poems here use rhymed stanzas throughout. Where possible, this has been suggested in the English, but a translation priority has been to correctly signal the best English equivalent of the word chosen rather than substitute one with a better rhyme.

The translator's art always involves selection among potential equivalences in the target language so as to most correctly reflect the original poem. An advantage of working with living poets is that occasionally we were able to consult with them to determine the intended images. For example, Daysi Flores writes "Los cascabeles olorosos a tormenta" ("Impotente" / "Impotent")—"The X smelling of storm." The noun *cascabel* in Honduran Spanish could be "bell," as in the Christmas carol, "Jingle Bell, Jingle Bell"; or "rattle," as in a baby's toy; or "rattlesnake," also the title of a successful 1998 novel by Guatemalan Arturo Arias; or a type of chili pepper and plant. Wikipedia provides other options: (artillery) name in English for a muzzle-loading cannon and pellet casing, as in the nursery rhyme, "Long John Silver went to sea / A cascabel upon his knee"; roller coaster name in Chapultepec Park in Mexico City; town in Arizona; and partial title of a novel by Jules Verne. Of these options, the only one obviously associated with fragrance is the chili pepper or plant, also logical in the context. But no, the poet replied that she was referring to rattles, and the translator chose: "Rattles smelling of storms." What a different image, had one of the alternatives been chosen!

In this sense, translations always involve choices, and vastly different translations can still be correct. One choice does not delegitimize others, but we have endeavored in all the translations to reflect the poet's sensitivity to word choice from among other options available to her in Spanish. With the bilingual format readers fluent in Spanish can immediately consult the original poem to enrich their reading and judge the appropriateness of the translation.

Lety Elvir, Editor
María Roof, Translation Editor

# ORGANIZATIONS AND ABBREVIATIONS

ANDEH: Asociación Nacional de Escritoras de Honduras
    National Association of Honduran Women Writers
CCET: Centro Cultural España en Tegucigalpa
    Spanish Cultural Center in Tegucigalpa
CDM: Centro de Derechos de la Mujer
    Women's Rights Center
CEM-H: Centro de Estudios de la Mujer–Honduras
    Women's Studies Center–Honduras
CIDH: Corte Interamericana de Derechos Humanos
    Inter-American Court of Human Rights
CIPRODEH: Centro de Investigación y Promoción de los Derechos Humanos
    Center for Human Rights Research and Promotion
CODEMUH: Colectiva de Mujeres Hondureñas
    Honduran Women's Collective
CODIMCA: Consejo para el Desarrollo Integral de la Mujer Campesina
    Council for the Integral Development of the Rural Woman
COFADEH: Comité de Familiares de Detenidos Desaparecidos en Honduras
    Committee of Relatives of Disappeared Detainees in Honduras
Colectivo Marxista Feminista Las Necias
    Las Necias/Women Fools Marxist Feminist Collective
COMPPA: Comunicadores Populares Por la Autonomía
    Popular Communicators for Autonomy
CONADEH: Comisionado Nacional de los Derechos Humanos en Honduras
    National Commission on Human Rights in Honduras
FATCA: Frente Amplio de Trabajadores(as) de la Cultura y el Arte
    Broad Front of Workers in Culture and Art
FEHMUC: Federación Hondureña de Mujeres Campesinas
    Honduran Federation of Rural Women
Feministas en Resistencia
    Feminists in Resistance

FNJR: Frente Nacional de Juventudes en Resistencia
   National Youths in Resistance Front
FNRP: Frente Nacional de Resistencia Popular
   National Popular Resistance Front
FRU: Frente de Reforma Universitaria
   University Reform Front
JASS: Asociadas por lo Justo
   Just Associates
JND: Juventud Nueva Democracia
   New Democracy Youth Movement
La Resistencia
   The Resistance
LGTB: Asociación LGTB Arcoiris de Honduras
   LGBT Rainbow Association of Honduras
LIBRE: Partido Libertad y Refundación
   LIBRE Party; Liberty and Refounding Party
LIMUPH: Liga de Mujeres Patriotas de Honduras
   League of Women Patriots of Honduras
MND: Movimiento Nueva Democracia
   New Democracy Movement
Movimiento Feminista de Honduras
   Feminist Movement of Honduras
Movimiento Poético Las de Hoy
   Women of Today Poetry Movement
OFRANEH: Organización Fraternal Negra de Honduras
   Black Fraternal Organization of Honduras
OPLN: Organización Política Los Necios/Las Necias-Honduras
   Los Necios/Las Necias (Men/Women Fools) Político
   Organizacton-Honduras
PaísPoesible
   PaísPoesible Poetry Collective
Red de Mujeres Jóvenes de Cortés
   Young Women of Cortés Network
Red Nacional de Defensoras de Derechos Humanos
   National Network of Women Human Rights Defenders
REDCAM: Red Centroamericana de Organizaciones de
   Mujeres en Solidaridad con las Trabajadoras de la Maquila
   Central American Network of Organizations of
   Women in Solidarity with Maquila Workers
RIEPA: Red Internacional de Editores y Proyectos Alternativos
   International Network of Alternative Editors and Projects

UEAH: Unión de Escritores y Artistas de Honduras
    Union of Writers and Artists of Honduras
UHE: Unión Hispanomundial de Escritores
    Hispanoworld Union of Writers
UNAH: Universidad Nacional Autónoma de Honduras
    National Autonomous University of Honduras
UPNFM: Universidad Pedagógica Nacional Francisco Morazán
    Francisco Morazán National Pedagogical University
UTH: Universidad Tecnológica de Honduras
    Technological University of Honduras

# PRESENTATION OF THE FIRST EDITION

*"These poems bring an urgency to speak; they bring the breeze, song, blood, pain, the time and hopes of a people attacked, where women also struggle, write, condone, condemn, and are reborn... and struggle again..., and write again."*

–L.E.

The June 28, 2009 coup d'état deeply marked the national conscience of Honduras, engaged the entire population, polarized Honduran society, and plunged to previously inconceivable depths the repression, insecurity, violation of the freedom of expression,[1] violence,[2] corruption and ungovernability of the country. Impunity is rampant, and confidence in institutions has crumbled; lack of protection from the persistent violation of human rights terrorizes society and, simultaneously, pushes it to struggle for an urgent change in the current state of affairs.

Women, a majority in our population, have demonstrated decisively, along with other sectors, against the coup d'état and other injustices; they have made their presence felt in several ways: by protesting in the streets, surviving

---

1 Honduras has seen 34 journalists murdered in the last four years, 28 of them during the administration of Porfirio Lobo Sosa (2010-2014), among them, two women, and more than 200 cases of attacks on freedom of expression in general; all these cases have enjoyed nearly total impunity, according to a June 25, 2013, report by the Committee of Relatives of Disappeared Detainees in Honduras (COFADEH).

2 The Coordinator of COFADEH reported slightly different figures, but the impact is strikingly similar: "During the Porfirio Lobo administration those murdered included 119 women, 53 lawyers, 35 journalists, 84 taxi drivers, dozens of community leaders [more than 186 from the LGTB community from the coup to May 2013, according to Kukulkán, in *La Tribuna*, May 18, 2013] and more than **100 farmers** fighting for their rights against local landowners. In fact, Honduras has the **highest percentage of homicides in the world.** It is the most violent country in Latin America, surpassing Mexico, and the poorest after Haiti. The rate of lethal crimes for each 100,000 inhabitants is 86, while the world average is 8.8. Several reports link certain police sectors to the activity of **death squads.** Despite this, the United States continues to provide economic assistance to the Honduran military and police forces and hold **joint U.S.-Honduras operations** against narcotrafficking. Recently in one of these operations four civilians were killed." Interview with Bertha Oliva, Coordinator of COFADEH. Source: http://www.eldiario.es/internacional/campana-electoral-Honduras-contienda-sangre_0_141735980.html.

repressions, recovering land, abandoning their traditional house-bound work to attend meetings, popular assemblies, takeovers of highways, lectures.... They have also protested through diverse artistic expressions, including graffiti, theater, music, cinema, dance, photography, painting, weavings, wall paintings, literature, etc. Nevertheless, the lack of studies and research on women's artistic production, contextualized in this historical moment, is evident.

Out of this necessity we developed the idea in 2010 to contribute a grain of sand to fill the gap, to compile a body of literature, poetry in this case, that would render it more visible and serve as a basis for national and international academic studies. But most especially, to leave historical evidence of the discourse of a people that in the voices and letters of women has said "Enough!" to so much oligarchical ignominy and advances with dignity toward its independence from neocolonialism

That idea is now concretized in the compilation and dialogue of 119 poems, written by 47 women[3] with clear positions of resistance to the coup d'état, its causes and consequences for Honduran society in general, and for women in particular. By recognizing the importance of this poetry, this thought, this discourse, and by disseminating them, we do justice to the authors, to women, subjects and decisive agents in the situation that Honduras currently faces.

It was difficult to compile this literary *corpus* because most of the poems had not been published and also because of the slow pace of submission and authorization for publication. The women in this book are very busy people whose time is filled with commitments and duties related to work, art, family and politics. Several of the texts were found through social media such as Facebook or web pages of The Resistance, like <www.voselsoberano.com>, and a very few had been published in books (see details in "Antecedents and Justification").

This anthology does not reflect all the women who wrote resistance poems, or all those who are in the resistance, even though the project of compiling the anthology was open,

---

3 In the edition in Spanish. This revised and augmented edition includes 131 poems by 53 women.

that is, for unpublished as well as published authors. It was advertised on radio and television, to email addresses and social media, at women's events and poetry recitals, book presentations and related cultural events, and the word was spread among women known and even well-known as poets.

Not everyone is here, because some writers continue to maintain their anonymity, and others did not learn of the project. Still others say they have been unable to write even one poem on the topic: "I am frozen, dry, I can't write about the coup; it has paralyzed me." More than one expressed fear of repression in the workplace or by the State, or by paramilitaries, and some feared literary criticism. Others had their "workshopped" poems lost, or, simply, the computers where they stored their writings were stolen. But, included are all the poets who were found, all the ones who sent one or more poems, with three being the maximum by each poet. All are important poets, because with their voices, they create resistance; with their resistance, they make poetry; with their poetry they also refound the nation.

The essay "Antecedents and Justification" outlines literary precedents for this collection, and an introductory study follows that was prepared at the beginning of the process, with a first sampling of the poems received, when this project was still just a seed.

I invite all of you to get to know, to read, to share these stories told as testimony, as analytical thought and social mobilization by these women gathered here who call out to others. I invite you to imagine that a better world is possible, a world that will be antipatriarchal, anti-imperialist, nonviolent, democratic and just.

Lety Elvir. Tegucigalpa, September 1, 2013.

## ANTECEDENTS AND JUSTIFICATION

Anthologies of poetry written by Honduran women have been so few and far between that the entire repertoire consists of only two: *Honduras: mujer y poesía. Antología de poesía escrita por mujeres (1865-1998)* (Honduras: Women and Poetry. Anthology of Poetry Written by Women [1865-1998]), published in Honduras in 1998 by Ada Luz Pineda, and *Poetry by Contemporary Honduran Women*, by Amanda Castro, published in the United States in a bilingual edition in 2002. Castro's anthology did not reach the Honduran market and costs $180 per copy–reasons why it was not acquired and is hardly known among the poets themselves.

In the political circumstances generated by the coup d'état of 2009,[1] literature by women has been abundant, but not always in written form.[2] Several books by male poets have been published,[3] in addition to two anthologies: the first contains only poetry and includes 17 men and 8 women;[4] the second is a collection of essays, articles and poetry, with poems by 11 men and 0 women.[5]

The reasons why women have not published their poems or gathered them in books[6] are many and diverse; for example, the lack of publishers interested in their work; lack of time, due to social and work roles assigned to the female gender; or fear of repression;[7] and, above all, lack of eco-

---

1 In prior coups, specifically that of 1963, Clementina Suárez (1902-1991), Sara Salazar (1946), and others repudiated those undemocratic acts in poems.

2 An important number of poems produced after the coup were available only orally, broadcast on programs at local radio stations: Radio Gualcho, Radio Progreso, Radio Uno, and Radio Globo, which was the only station with national coverage that denounced the coup and allowed people to call in and read their poems without identifying themselves out of fear of State repression. Those poems are difficult to find and save. Apparently tapes were not kept.

3 Óscar Espinal, Candelario Reyes, Alberto Destephen, Víctor Manuel Ramos.

4 Merlo, Melissa and Israel Serrano (compilers and editors). *Poesía hondureña en resistencia* (Honduran Poetry in Resistance), Tegucigalpa: Verbo Editores/Argos Editores, October 2009.

5 Serrano, Israel, Melissa Merlo and Víctor Manuel Ramos. *Honduras sendero en Resistencia* (Honduras Path in Resistance), Tegucigalpa: Verbo Editores, June 2010.

6 Except: Guifarro, Blanca. *Versos en resistencia* (Verses in Resistance), Tegucigalpa, 2009; *Para no olvidar* (So As Not to Forget), Tegucigalpa, 2011.

7 As of January 2013, the level of violent deaths in Honduras has reached 92 per 100,000 inhabitants, according to organisms that record violence and those that defend human rights. The year 2012 ended with the figure of at least 600 women murdered. Many of these people belonged to the National Popular Resistance Front (FNRP), according to statements by families and friends. Nearly 100% of these cases have gone unpunished.

nomic resources to self-finance publications.⁸

In this sense, it is necessary, urgent, and fair to continue efforts to make visible the literary production by women, particularly poetry written during and after the coup, which is the focus of this book.

The publication of this anthology surely will not be appreciated by certain sectors and by the *golpistas*—people who promoted or are linked to the coup; it could lead to certain risks. The authors included here are aware of this situation and are willing to publish their work in the current conditions, but within their personal possibilities. For this reason, two of the poets selected in the first sample obtained in October 2010 appear here under pseudonyms, at their request.⁹

The anthology appears in an election year. On November 24, 2013, general elections will be held to elect a new administration that will govern the direction of the Honduran State for the next four years (January 27, 2014 to January 27, 2018). According to analysts and organisms defending human rights, it is anticipated that before the elections, increases will be seen in the number of political murders and level of violence and of criminality in general. The fear of electoral fraud against the Liberty and Refounding Party, LIBRE,[10] which is the political arm of the National Popular Resistance Front, and in favor of the conservative and *golpista* political parties, will be inevitable in the current circumstances. And if this happens, if fraud materializes, the reaction of the affected sectors could manifest itself in diverse scenes of resistance, where the repression intended to crush that resistance would be colossal. Nevertheless, art, poetry and women writers will also be there, to continue making and writing history.

Lety Elvir. Tegucigalpa, May 2013.

---

8 Almost 50% of the economically active population is un- or underemployed, according the official sources at the Ministry of Labor.

9 As of May 31, 2013, when this section was last updated, one of the poets has left the country to reside elsewhere, although another poet, under similar conditions, joined the anthology, so the number of poets using false names or pseudonyms remains the same.

10 The FNRP decided to undertake the political struggle and participate in the electoral process by forming the political party LIBRE in October 2011, after the effort to reinstate President José Manuel Zelaya Rosales failed, and subsequent to his return to Honduras in May 2011 after nearly two years of exile in the Dominican Republic, and after the signing of the Cartagena Accord. LIBRE, a leftist party that seeks to break the traditional two-party control, as well as to effect a refounding of the Honduran State, selected as presidential candidate for the 2013 elections Xiomara Castro Sarmiento, wife of the deposed president.

# INTRODUCTION

## "Poetry Written by Women and the Coup d'État in Honduras, 2009"[1]

### Lety Elvir

*"We are that entity being sold to us (...). We are the nation! I have always thought that Honduras has a woman's name."*
—Juana Pavón[2]

Honduras: June 28, 2009, a military-oligarchy coup d'état, organized by a transnational genocidal conspiracy, destroys the inchoate democracy beginning to take shape under the administration of President Manuel Zelaya Rosales and quashes hope that the nation is heading toward better times.

But with the coup came the birth of what is now known as the National Popular Resistance Front, the FNRP, originally called the National Front of Resistance against the Coup d'État. A social and political movement like this has never been seen before in Honduras, with nothing similar perhaps since the great Banana Workers Strike of 1954, and it unites the most democratic and antimilitary sectors of the country, in which the majority of participants are women. Women joined men and took to the streets to define new aspirations and create a new nation, women and men who marched to resist the state of terror that was instituted from that first day forward and denounce the coup with cries of "No blows against the State, no blows against women!" and "We are not

---

1 Earlier versions of this essay were presented at the 3rd Central American Congress on Cultural Studies, Los Angeles, sponsored by California State University, Northridge, June 2-5, 2011, and at the 2nd Encounter of Central American Women Authors, Managua, Nicaragua, November 17-18, 2010.

2 Juana Pavón (Honduras, 1945), author of the poetry collection, *Yo soy esa sujeto* (I Am That Subject, San Pedro Sula, Editorial Capiro, 1994). The poem, "Nosotras, esas sujetos" (We, Those Subjects), from which the epigraph is taken, is dated 1986, when Central America was bleeding to death from civil wars. In Honduras, social and political movements demanded the closing of the U.S. military base on our sovereign soil, and this poem became an omnipresent symbol at anti-imperialist protests and political rallies in the capital and other cities.

afraid. *Golpistas*, leave!"³

Thus begins a new phase in the history of a country in that Central America fragmented by ignoble interests: a country whose name is associated with intrigues and coups against fellow states and their democracies; called the "backyard," the United States' aircraft carrier in Central America, and "Banana Republic"; a land militarily occupied by four foreign armies in the decade of the 1980s: the Nicaraguan "Contras"—counterrevolutionaries, the Army of El Salvador, the U.S. Army, with its military base in Palmerola (used as the center of operations for the coup), and the Army of Honduras, which is not really "of Honduras," since it serves the interests of imperialist powers and local groups with de facto power.

This country's people have had to tolerate labels like "cowardly," "submissive," "conservative," "forgetful," "lazy," "hardly human, wearing loincloths," because this is how the gentlemen who have taken over Honduras and Central America want us to be known. These characterizations were confirmed by psychological, cultural and anthropological studies on our way of being and echoed by their sciences and scientists. They were to be believed because they said it and so-called "specialists" repeated it, despite the history of rebellion by the Honduran people, despite the Hondurans who were disappeared, incarcerated, murdered, tortured, persecuted, exiled and victimized by the dictatorship in power, which did not, and does not, forgive the "sin" of dissidence and opposition.

We could ask: If Honduras is a small, poor country, with only 112,492 km² /43,278 sq. mi. of land and eight million inhabitants, for what reason and for what purpose would you inflict a coup d'état on it in the 21st century? Because its geographical location is in a zone considered strategic in international military geopolitics and likewise strategic for globalized neoliberalism. Honduras is one more vote in

---

3 Translator's note: "¡Ni golpes de Estado, ni golpes a las mujeres!" illustrates a multivalent use of the word "golpe," which means a punch, hit, blow, strike, as a fighter would inflict, and also is the "coup" in coup d'état. Plays on the multiple meanings of this word appear in several poems here. Since English has no good word for "golpista"— derived from the Spanish "golpe de Estado," to name a person who executes or supports a coup d'état, and to describe such action, we have kept the term *golpista*.

international organizations of nations to promote invasions and imperialist wars, to block the liberation of other countries, and to besiege the riches and minds of the people of the world.

It is no coincidence that immediately after the coup the National Congress of Honduras approved and continues to approve treaties and laws that allow the installation of more U.S. military bases in Honduran territory, in addition to the expansion of the military base at Palmerola. One new base is in the Mosquito Coast area bordering Nicaragua, another in the Bay Islands in the Caribbean, and these are not the only ones.

It is no coincidence that laws have been repealed and others passed in order to deny the rights of women to make decisions regarding their bodies, health and sexual reproduction, upon the initiative of fundamentalist religious groups that are in collusion with power and are in positions of de facto institutional power.

It is no coincidence that in November 2009, in the midst of citizens' protests, unbridled repression and a terror campaign against the population, the *golpistas* carried out an electoral process in order to legitimize and consolidate their coup and to export the idea that everything had been settled in Honduras. Meanwhile, the deposed president, Manuel Zelaya Rosales, remained in asylum at the Brazilian Embassy in Tegucigalpa, where he had been since September 21, when he entered the country clandestinely to seek a dialogue for his reinstatement and the reestablishment of constitutional order.

Of course, there was no reinstatement, just more repression, and President Zelaya could not leave the Brazilian Embassy until January 27, 2010, when the *golpistas* allowed him to depart directly into exile on the very day of the inauguration of the new government that was declared the winner in the false elections of November 2009 and that embodied a continuation of the coup d'état.

It is no coincidence that since the coup, laws have been passed that allow the usurpation of rivers for hydroelectric dams, laws that allow the leasing, sale and concessions of large swaths of Honduran territory for the installation of maquila assembly plant enclaves and zones free of any control by the Honduran State. New laws allow enclaves of petroleum and mining companies that will pay neither taxes nor the true price of the oil, silver and other important metals and precious gemstones, much less the labor of an unemployed people left without rights or protections, because the laws that favored them have been repealed or ignored since the coup.

It is no coincidence, then, that an international media war has disinformed and misled its audience, its respective populations, leading them to almost totally abandon protest and international solidarity with the Honduran people living with defenselessness, impunity for wrongdoers and repression. This, to such an extent that the United Nations has declared Honduras the most violent country in the world, with 91.4 intentional homicides for each 100,000 inhabitants in 2011.

It is no coincidence, then, that artistic production in Honduras is imbued with this historical moment and with the committed positioning, assumed by the immense majority of writers and artists in general, in favor of a re-founding of the nation.

This is the context in which women writers become the chroniclers, singers, songwriters and troubadours of their time: the poets themselves are the witnesses and protagonists in this historical moment. In the midst of poisonous gases, clubs, bullets, rapes, deaths and new hopes, they build a better world with their bodies and their writings through militancy in the popular resistance.

This essay, then, focuses on women and their poetic production after the 2009 coup d'état and seeks to compile and disseminate the testimony of Honduran women poets expressed in verses, composed of many voices, wrenched from personal and non-personal experience, from suffering and joy in the struggle against the dictatorial regime in order to recover their dignity.[4] I also attempt to analyze the role of poetry as a "'combat arm' against authority and official

---

4 The poets and poems analyzed here are a small sampling of the unpublished, spontaneous poetic production after June 28, 2009. The entire literary production cannot be compiled at this time because, among other reasons, many women who wrote and write poetry must maintain their anonymity, and some poets disseminated their poems orally through alternative radio stations, the only ones allowing comments on the coup d'état.

history,"⁵ as trench work and flag in the time of war against an unarmed, undefended people, in the time of this struggle where the impact of women and men poets in the resistance is obviously deep.

I am especially interested in reading and sharing what the women poets are feeling, experiencing and saying about the crisis generated by the coup, how they have spoken and are speaking about it. In fact, the poems themselves answer these and other questions, so I believe it is most important to share them, to make them and their authors visible and publish these stories in verse.

This is not exactly an essay of literary criticism, but rather a text intended to help break the silence. It is a small part of the historical story that will not be written or narrated by the owners of the mass media, who are themselves *golpistas* and owners of this country.

Here are the poems, then, as they were sent to my email address, or as I found them in online publications, on social media or in blogs of alternative and Resistance media on the internet.⁶ I present these poems with no intention of judging them for their aesthetic value or anything of that nature. I am interested in the poems principally as historical products or constructs, as literary discourses, spoken witnesses of a social praxis.

Jéssica Sánchez (Jéssica Isla) (1974). Her poem, "PRESENTATION," speaks to us, among other themes, of the individual beaten body, simultaneously identified with the collective body of the dissident multitude that becomes one body, everyone's, one body that walks peacefully singing chants down rural and urban streets, one body that runs and flees from the military and militarized police that beats them, pursues them and fires murdering bullets; one body

---

5 The phrase is from Marie-Louise Ollé's chapter, "Testimonio y estética o cómo (re) presentar el horror" (Testimony and Aesthetics, or How to [Re]present the Horror), in *Voces del silencio. Literatura y Testimonio en Centroamérica* (Voices of Silence. Literature and Testimony in Central America), compiled by José Domingo Carrillo and Lucrecia Méndez de Penedo (Aguascalientes, Mexico: Universidad Autónoma, 2006), pp. 397-416.

6 This introductory essay makes reference only to poems I had compiled by May 2011. In the anthology section of this book, these and poems received later are reproduced in their entirety.

made up of many bodies capable of painting signs or walls and dancing in the midst of the terror unleashed by those in olive green uniforms. A body that resists and presents itself because it has a desire—a desire for revolution.

### PRESENTATION
I am this body drawn by blows
that walks day after day under the sun,
under this uncertain sky of winged machines,
amid blasts of smoke and
the sound of rifles.
I am countless faces: (...)
who confront in groups or all together
olive green walls charged with violence

I can say many smells leave my body
of fresh montuca
of tortilla and beans (...)
the smell of blood shed (...)
   I am the resistance.
         *August 2009*

Diana Espinal (1964). In "Lazarus Rises" we find Diana's version of what has happened in Honduras since the coup—militarization of Honduran society against a people which, despite the fear provoked by that militarization, like the Biblical Lazarus awakes and rises up against an "unacceptable state."

### Lazarus Rises
(...)
Swarms of boots and an unacceptable state of cloudbursts
offer downpours to the wind (...)

Today the twenty-first century asks to be suckled
Lazarus rose with his robes of ants
someone takes out his old beads of ground glass
someone coagulates the cry of hinges

In the dispensing of fear
are hemorrhages that violate dreams.

Mayra Oyuela (1982). Her poetry since the coup has undertaken a deeper social and aesthetic reflection that places each word as a piece of evidence, as a wound, where irony, transparency and commitment to the country and its people cannot be absent. For example, the poem "Our Voice Raised in Protest Obligates Us (or Shameless Rhetoric)" denounces for all the world to see what happened on June 28, 2009, as the poet also raises her arm and points her index finger at the symbol of empire and god of money, New York, with its Wall Street and its metro full of rats, the Statue of Liberty and Ground Zero where the Twin Towers stood before 9-11.

**Our Voice Raised in Protest Obligates Us
(or Shameless Rhetoric)**
Good morning unions, good morning socialists (...),
Welcome rats, welcome sun,
welcome stone, grackles, pseudo human rights
cudgels and stool pigeons:
We are gathered together here today
because as of this morning a cockroach
governs in the presidential palace.
Comrades who are language purists,
I make no excuses for my rhetoric
because the cesspools of New York
have incited bloodshed (...)
We will not kneel,
this is not the time to pray.
We will not wait for them to crucify our belief
that we can breathe life into new democracies (...)
We who stand guard over dreams through empty nights
will not intrude on the weeping of mothers who build
                                                the country
with the names of their dead sons and daughters.

Amanda Castro (1962-2010) was a poet who knew the importance of words, whose verses denounced the violent nature of the history of Latin American peoples, a woman unafraid to lay out her political and ideological positions in her literature, along with her sexual preferences, and her commitment to feminism and to women's literature. A crafter of words, she was a great warrior who, in clinging to her oxygen tank, clung to life, and that did not prevent her from participating in the hunger strike and many other protests against the coup. Amanda fought with words and body against the coup regime until her dying days.

**Words Are Good For...**
What good are/ these stupid words of mine/ that murmur from the Profound/ void/ (...) spending the whole day scanning information/ checking it/ to put in a blog/ that maybe only 30 people will read/ in the whole world/ what good is it?/ I wonder/
(...)
Words are good/ for re/knowing and recognizing ourselves/ and identi/fying ourselves/ and knowing ourselves to be/ brothers and sisters/ compas[7] in the struggle/ –because sitting in silence/ is also to struggle–/ and see how we are finding each other/ in networks that don't even exist (...) and count/ the steps that march/ quickly/ while shots are fired/ the sacred backdrop/ and the pale Blue/ (...)

Words/ are good/ are good/ merely for mentioning the Hondura/ that lies/ wounded and bloody/ waiting/ waiting for you/
*(July 28, 2009/ one month in resistance)*

Karla Lara (1968) has been well-known since the 1980s as a singer with an exceptional voice that she puts at the service of poems written by others. But Karla also writes songs; she writes poetry and sings it. Like the immense majority of women writers and artists, Karla stands in resistance to the post-coup regime that continues coup values. Her poem, "A Manuel" tenderly describes Manuel Flores, a teacher who also wrote and fought against the coup and the capitalist system that refused to forgive his daring dissidence, and its thugs murdered him on March 23, 2010.

---

[7] "compas," abbreviation of "compañeros," meaning colleagues, companions, like-minded people, buddies.

### To Manuel

*(Manuel Flores, a teacher who was murdered in front of his students at the high school where he worked. He was a member of the Socialist Party of Central America.)*

You took it to the streets
and sowed ideas, Manuel
bandana around your neck,
bag over your shoulder, Manuel (...)

You were so tall,
and your leftist heart so large, Manuel
you were like some hippy
or like sweet Jesus himself, Manuel

They chant in the streets
it´s your name they chant, Manuel
and in our school and in our barrio
we miss you so much, Manuel.
 *(2010)*

Blanca Guifarro (1946), sociologist, writer and feminist, assumed a commitment to popular struggles from an early age and founded the Women's Studies program at the National Autonomous University of Honduras (UNAH). After June 28, 2009, her poems were among the first to circulate from hand to hand at protest mobilizations, political rallies and bookstores. She has written poems to several members of the Resistance who were murdered. Isi [Isis, Isy] Obed Murillo, 19 years of age, is considered the first martyr of the Resistance, killed by an Armed Forces sniper's bullet on July 5, 2009, at the Toncontín Airport, where he was part of the crowd awaiting the return of deposed President Manuel Zelaya Rosales, who was not allowed to land. Wendy Ávila, a university student, died in 2010 as a result of poisoning from tear gas. During a protest by teachers on March 17, 2011, professor Ilse Ivania Velásquez died of multiple contusions from the impact of a grenade that exploded in her face and being run over by a car whose driver was fleeing police repression in a blinding cloud of tear gas.

Blanca's poem "White House Hunt in Three Acts" makes a clear allusion to an imperialist symbol, the White House, home to United States presidents, where conversation is not just about children's stories and lullabies, or university interns' coats, but also about coups d'état and other military topics. Blanca writes "casa," house, with a "z" instead of an "s" to make it "caza," hunt, to compare it to hunting by a clawed animal that rips apart lives and destroys people.

**White House Hunt in Three Acts**
act I
I have seen
sadness penetrate
in each body without a body
skeletons (...)

act II
you cannot control
your endless ambition (...)

act III
an experienced chameleon
you go
where you aren't invited (...)

"Isabel Rivera" is a pseudonym requested by a Honduran poet who fears reprisals if her political position is known. She dedicates her poem to the journalist Jorge Orellana, better known as "Georgino," who was killed by a bullet to the head as he was leaving his television program one night in April 2010.

## The Day Georgino Was Killed
*(In honor of the journalist Jorge Orellana)*

Under the bush of impunity
a coup blow to ideas
a bullet shot by ambition
that was not made of rubber.

A blow to the heart
they shattered the utopia of a fairer country
a broken family. (...)
Sorrows are often infinite.

Iris Mencía (1959) wrote the poem "Hopes," in which she establishes our ancient roots of rebellion. Without mentioning names, she alludes to the heroic struggle led by Lempira and other indigenous people who resisted Spanish colonization. Reconnecting with ancestral knowledge and ritual, Iris speaks of hope renewed by the rebirth of struggle by an impoverished people that now also dreams of itself and rebels.

## Hopes

Consciousness
rises again (...)
without disguise
from ancient lineage (...)
advances
penetrates cities without wavering
voices burn
like resin and candles (...)
not waiting
hope captures
even shoeless feet
          September 2010[8]

---

[8] The poem used in this essay was not later included in the anthology. The original poem is:
**Esperanzas**
Renace
sin disimulos

Diana E. Vallejo (1969) denounces and upbraids the role played by different institutions, such as the Church and the Congress, to thwart the awakening of the Honduran people, which clearly knows how to identify its enemies and rises to take ownership of its own destiny.

**The People**
(...)
Vultures encircle an amputated, withered Congress
(...)
The churches of the Middle Ages have returned
cold, macabre, more dangerous
salaried assassins.

No one is burned at the stake,
but blood is boiled at gun point (...)

But today we
run the show (...)
No one will again sing to entertain the master.
We are the master...
   3-31-2011

Lety Elvir (1966). A fateful date in the history of the always-weak Honduran democracy was October 21, 1956, when the Armed Forces executed a coup d'état and thereby ensured the autonomy of that institution and its takeover of State control. They also ensured that this date was included in the calendar of national celebrations and holidays. On October 21, 2009, during the evolution of another coup, pro-

---

   la consciencia
   desde una antigua estirpe
   avanza
   sin vértigo penetra en las ciudades
   las voces arden
   como copal y candelas
   no aguarda
   la esperanza atrapa
   hasta los pies descalzos
      *Septiembre de 2010*

moted by the same interests and similar actors, this poem was born that denounces it, its polarizations, horrors and aspirations.

### Dotting Some I's Regarding the Coup
*These dead men, these dead women, have fled from death,*
   *the assassins can never flee from their victims*
   *though they disclaim remorse and blame.*

And from the caves they emerged
with decrees and machine guns
with pronouncements and clubs
with dogs and chains
with cynicisms and lies
with gases and tanks...
and came here. (...)

And despite so much spilled blood (...)
this people rises, walks and marches
into the 21$^{st}$ century
resists, grows angry and sings
rescues Honduras
and renews the world.
   *(October 21, 2009)*


## A CONCLUSION

A coup d'état against the Honduran people took place, and since then, we are living in a permanent state of coups d'état. There was and there is resistance by the people, resistance that appears in all its dimensions and forms, through words, poetry, essays, chants, painting, music, masks, spray painting, graffiti, banners, signs, photography, murals, slingshots, films, theater, etc. Here is an artistic Spring that denounces, points fingers, speaks out, mocks the *golpistas* and makes a significant contribution to the development of a social class consciousness that understands that the purpose of this coup d'état has been to seize more of our resources and everything that sparks "that sensation of tenderness that money produces," as a poem by Roberto Sosa puts it.[9]

This poetic sampling written by Honduran women is just a drop in the ocean of what was provoked and produced after the coup. People in Honduras, their mentalities, arts, politics and History have changed since then; something was broken forever and for the better. Overall, poetry written by women in this historical moment positions itself resoundingly against this economic, criminal, patriarchal, exclusionary, militaristic system and proposes (and acts and participates and decides in favor of) the re-founding of the country, to rescue the nation and build a State of Law that advances toward social justice, toward a just distribution of riches, toward the construction of the happiness of its citizenry. And this poetry and its authors know that this is not a utopia; they know its dawn is coming.

Tegucigalpa, October 31, 2010, and May 31, 2011.

---

[9] Honduran poet Roberto Sosa (1930- 2011).

Women's Poems of Protest and Resistance

## Honduras, 2009-2014

## SOLEDAD ALTAMIRANO
### (Lejamaní, Comayagua, 1962)

**PENA**

*A Milko Durán Céspedes*

No sé dónde esconder
esta vergüenza,
si la dejo bajo las piedras,
las mismas piedras
tendrán vergüenza,
no sé qué hacer
para retribuirle a Milko
todo este dolor
esta humillación
y este daño que le han hecho.
Ahora que
"Tegucigalpa está de moda"
que no esperen los golpistas
que vendrán turistas
para que los traten
como lo han hecho con Milko,
quería, solamente quería
llevarse todo lo bello
que Honduras tiene,
en cambio se lleva
una etapa triste y dura
de su vida.

**SOLEDAD ALTAMIRANO**

Graduate in Letters and teacher in the Department of Languages and Literature, Francisco Morazán National Pedagogical University (UPNFM). Diplomas in Higher Education and in Research and Administrative Computer Technology; Master's in Central American Literature, National Autonomous University (UNAH). Poems selected for national and international anthologies. Participant in recitals and other cultural events in several countries, including Chile, Mexico, Puerto Rico, El Salvador and Guatemala. Book of poetry, *Cronología de una ausencia* (Chronology of an Absence, 2001).

**SHAME**
    *For Milko Durán Céspedes**

I don't know where to hide
this lament,
if I leave it under stones
the very stones
will feel shame,
what do I do
to make up to Milko
for all this pain
this humiliation
and this damage they have done.
Now that
"Tegucigalpa is stylish"
don't think, you *golpistas*,
tourists will come here
to be treated
as you treated Milko,
who wanted, only wanted,
to remember all the beautiful things
Honduras has,
but instead he takes home
a sad and cruel time
in his life.

---

* A Venezuelan Colombian visitor to Honduras who was arrested, tortured and illegally detained in August 2009.

**Quedan**
> *A Allan McDonald*

Quedan solamente
el humo de las bombas,
el ruido de los cristales rotos,
el grito ahogado de los muertos,
la sangre en las calles,
las llagas en los pies,
el zumbido de las piedras,
el llanto forzado por las bombas lacrimógenas,
y el llanto por la impotencia ante la represión,
y este dolor por tu ausencia
que me golpea,
como tolete al escudo.
Mis lágrimas
brotan tan espontáneamente
cada vez que pienso que
te fuiste al exilio,
quisiera que te llevaras
la luz de una galaxia,
la esperanza de otro vuelo.
Te recordaré en la ráfaga
de cada amanecer.

**What's Left**
> *For Allan McDonald**

Smoke from the bombs
is all that is left,
the sound of breaking glass,
the strangled cry of the dead,
the blood in the streets,
the open wounds on our feet,
the zinging of stones,
the tears the gas made us weep,
the crying out impotent before repression
and this aching from your absence
that beats me
like a cudgel on a shield.
My tears
fall unbidden
every time I think of
your exile,
I wish you could take with you
a galaxy of light,
the hope of another flight.
I will remember you in the bright burst
of every dawn.


[*Translations by Janet N. Gold*]

---

* Award-winning Honduran political cartoonist, harassed by the military during the 2009 coup.

## SUYAPA ANTÚNEZ CERRATO
### (Tegucigalpa, 1965)

**Abran paso que yo ahí voy**<sup>*</sup>

Amigos vengo a contarles
lo que a mí me sucedió
por andar en resistencia
una macaneada me gané yo
y como no tengo miedo
yo les digo la verdad
por eso y muchas razones
me han querido hasta matar
bin voy, tin voy, abran paso que yo ahí voy
allá arriba venden coco
y allá abajo chicharrones
en la cabeza de los golpistas
hacen nido los ratones
de las muelas del alcalde
sabiéndolas cincelar
bien sale un par de dados
y una bola de billar

---

* Este escrito es canción con ritmo *ranchero*.

## SUYAPA ANTÚNEZ CERRATO

Gum and candy vendor in Tegucigalpa's Central Park. Mother of 4 girls and 3 boys. Along with her sales basket, she carries a notebook in her apron with her poems and protest songs and a ballpoint pen, in case inspiration comes while she's working. In July 2010, for being part of the Resistance and reciting contestatory poems, she was the victim of a brutal police beating that put her in the hospital for several days and left her partially blind in her left eye. Her poem, "We Poor Also Have Value," was published on January 25, 2011, in the *Tiempo* newspaper.

Translator's note: The English versions attempt to reflect the originals' sense of rhythm and rhyme. Occasionally, words chosen for this reason are not close translations. The tenor of the poems is unchanged.

### Make Way, I'm Coming Through!*

My friends, I'm here to tell you
what happened once to me
I stood with the resistance
and took a beating, you see,
and since I'm not afraid of them
and speak the truth with no dread
for that and other reasons
they want to make me dead
but here I am, but here I am, make way, I'm coming through
up there they sell coco
down here it's crispy pork rinds
in the heads of the *golpistas*
mice make nests in their minds
from the teeth of the mayor
using a chisel tool
you can make a pair of dice
and a ball for playing pool

---

* Lyrics for a song with a Mexican *ranchero* beat.

bin voy, tin voy, abran paso que yo ahí voy
cuando quieran trabajar
no vayan a la alcaldía
porque ahí sólo hallarán ladrones y policías
y si buscás un ladrón,
en la alcaldía
en el congreso
y en casa presidencial
hay un montón, montón, montón
bin voy, tin voy, abran paso que yo ahí voy
ya con esta me despido por las muelas de un zorrillo
y tengo las esperanzas
que este país
siempre va a ser mío
¡de todos los pobres!
bin voy, tin voy
abran paso que yo ahí voy.

but here I am, but here I am, make way, I'm coming through
when you want to get a job
don't go to city hall
cause the only thing you'll find there's
cops and robbers, that's all
but if you want to find a thief
try the mayor's office, or in a crunch,
halls of congress and president's house
where there's a bunch, bunch, bunch.
but here I am, but here I am, make way, I'm coming through
so now I'll end my tale
with everything I hope for
may this country always belong to me
and to all of us, the poor!
but here I am, but here I am
make way, I'm coming through.

**Delincuentes Uniformados***

Conozco delincuentes en esta ciudad
andan uniformados qué barbaridad
se creen dueños del mundo y de la Capital
son unos ignorantes, lástima me dan
son unos ladrones, grandes asesinos
matan y roban sin pensar. [Coro].

Además de todo eso les voy a aclarar
que a ellos los preparan para robar y matar
hagamos lo que hagamos
van a continuar
gaseando, toleteando y asaltando
a los que venimos a protestar
ya es demasiado, no los aguantamos,
nos van a cansar.

Conozco delincuentes en esta ciudad... [se repite el coro].

---

* Este escrito es para canción con ritmo *rock and roll.*

## Crooks in Uniform*

[Chorus] I know crooks in actuality
crooks in uniform, pure brutality
think they own the world and capital city
they're so ignorant, I feel sorry for them
these thieves and big murderers
who kill and rob without pity.

Besides all this, I've got to explain
that they're trained to kill & rob & maim
no matter what we try to do
them, they'll always be the same
teargasing, beating, assaulting too
like when to protest we came
it's too much, we won't take it,
there's no way they'll make us tame.

I know crooks in actuality... [repeat chorus]

---
* Lyrics for a rock & roll song.

**Para los que se venden en silencio**

Yo les vengo a decir
la merita verdad
y a los que no les guste
me van a disculpar.
Yo no soy reportera, tampoco periodista.
No soy ni profesora,
mucho menos ministra.
Yo no soy locutora, tampoco comentarista.
Soy una mujer sincera, honrada
y yo no me vendería
como lo hace la mayoría
de locutores, camarógrafos,
dirigentes, soldados y periodistas.
Y si por eso no me quieren
le doy gracias a Dios
si por la verdad murió Cristo
con gusto moriría yo.

## For Those Who Silently Sell Out

I've come here to say to you
God's honest truth be told
those of you who don't like it
no grudge to me can hold.
I'm no reporter, journalist either.
Professor,
state minister,
or newscaster, neither.
I'm a sincere and honest woman
and no sell-out will I be
like most
news & film producers
leaders, soldiers, journalists—not me.
I'll give thanks to God
if they don't like what I do
cause if Christ died for the truth
Me, I would gladly die too.


[*Translations by María Roof*]

## SUNY DEL CARMEN ARRAZOLA
### (Tegucigalpa, 1989)

**(En el futuro)**

En el futuro
si esta guerra no termina
seguiremos leyendo marxismo aunque no esté de moda.
Quizá nos convirtamos
en un montón de viejas torpes
que proyecten su amargura en el café de la tarde.
Si logramos ver
la última flor con vida
es probable que perdamos por completo la cordura
o, al contrario, abracemos el cénit de la dicha
convulsas, contemplando un último sol tibio
un último gramo de aire limpio
una última sonrisa en algún niño.

Por ahora, aquí estamos.
En el fondo del espanto
donde el cultivo de lo insólito
es el pan de cada día.
Donde, en su desorden, las luces
de la ciudad parecen
inválidas estrellas que no supieron volar.
Donde la sangre y las metrallas
son piezas de decorado público.
Donde el que calla, por miedo,
se encierra en un limbo de su propia construcción,

## SUNY DEL CARMEN ARRAZOLA

Degree in Letters, National Autonomous University (UNAH). Poems published in the anthology *Honduras-Chile* (2012) and in local newspapers and journals. First Prize in the Poetry Competition of the 10th "Visitación Padilla" University Art Encounter, 2010; second place in the Story Competition, 8th "Juan Ramón Molina" University Art Encounter, 2008.

### (In the Future)

In the future
if this war doesn't end
we'll still read Marxism, even if it's not in style.
Maybe we'll become
a bunch of awkward old ladies
projecting their bitterness in the afternoon coffee.
If we come to see
the last living flower
we'll probably lose our minds completely
or, the opposite, embrace the zenith of joy
excited, contemplating the last warm sun
the last gram of clear air
the last smile of a child.

For now, here we are.
In the depths of terror
where the cultivation of the unbelievable
is our daily bread.
Where, in disorder, the lights
of the city seem
invalid stars that knew not how to fly.
Where blood and guns
are parts of public decoration.
Where he who falls silent, out of fear,
shuts himself up in a limbo of his own making,

y aquel que no lo hace
engruesa la lista de mártires en el periódico.

Por ahora, así estamos,
viviendo con una abrumadora normalidad anormal
la crudeza de muerte
en este país triste
en esta ruta invisible

en lo hondo,
Honduras.

and he who doesn't
swells the list of martyrs in the newspaper.

For now, we are this way,
living with overwhelming abnormal normality
the indecency of death
in this sad country
on this invisible path

in the depths,
deeply Honduran.

**Memoria**

Los matorrales aun
guardan olor a ceniza.

Se siente el agua gotear
desde un cielo estampado:
no sabemos si es sangre, lluvia ácida o gritos
amarrados al semen de tarántulas verdes.

Hordas que se confunden
con toda la basura.
Ráfagas que ya no duelen
o duelen demasiado:
nos ensartan con furia esta escena perpetua
de guadañas rampantes.
...lentamente clavamos nuestros ojos al fango,
al abismo del suelo:
Arte del avestruz.

Sus golpes solo sacuden el fuego que nos calcina
golpes que arrinconaron la luz bajo sus corazas
golpes, con el poder de la muerte legislando
golpes que despertaron del sueño a la Memoria.

Y no dormiremos más
hasta rearmar los pedazos
por cada día con hambre,
por quienes antes soñaron y hoy tiñen los matorrales
el pueblo que un día fuimos...

Los que siempre estarán en ninguna parte.

**Memory**

The bushes still
smell of ashes.

Water is felt dripping
from a patterned sky:
we don't know if it's blood, acid rain or screams
tied to the semen of green tarantulas.

Mobs mixed in
with all the trash.
Bursts that no longer hurt
or hurt too much:
furiously string on us this perpetual scene
of rampant scythes.
... slowly we rivet our eyes on the mud,
the ground's abyss:
Art of the ostrich.

Their blows only stir the fire that chars us
blows that cornered light under their shields
blows, with the power of death legislating
blows that awoke Memory from its sleep.

And we shall sleep no more
til we reassemble the pieces
for each day of hunger
for those who dreamed before and today dye the bushes
the people we once were...

Those who will forever be nowhere.

## Utopía o muerte

> *"Lucho/ porque sé/ que algún día/*
> *el más grande crimen/ será pisar una flor"*
> —Julio San Francisco

Conozco la forma de tu silueta desde la sombra misma,
desde el volcán y el nido,
desde el bosque recóndito en tu propia mente;
te conozco
y hoy puedo jurar, compañera,
que esta trinchera que fundamos
no bajará su guardia frente a los truenos;
ni caerá ante la barbarie
este amor no profesado.

Quizás te vea o no te vea nunca,
quizás te mueras o muera en la lucha
pero la flor seguirá brillando
abierta a un nuevo norte
y las palomas volverán al parque
como vuelven a los prados
y al monte verde y escarpado.

Sé
que tras las paredes cercadas
y las líneas fronterizas
se halla esa libertad, lejana de las sombras.
Sé que amaré de nuevo este azul
que hoy me sabe a destierro
y que brillará un día el sol
como la Patria socialista.

Se predicará en las calles
el evangelio de la liberación,
mientras crezcan en los campos
los niños como granos de maíz.

**Utopia or Death**

> *"I struggle / because I know / that one day/
> the worst crime / will be to tread on a flower."*
> —Julio San Francisco

I know the form of your silhouette from the shadow itself,
from the volcano and the nest,
from the deep forest in your own mind;
I know you
and today I can swear, *compañera*,*
that his trench that we dug
will not lower its guard in the face of thunderclaps;
nor will this unprofessed love
fall to barbarity.

Perhaps I'll see you or not see you ever,
perhaps you will die or I will die
but the flower will continue to shine
open to a new direction
and the pigeons will return to the park
as to the meadows
and the green mountain and hillside.

I know
that behind fenced walls
and border lines
is that freedom, far from shadows.
I know I will again love this blue
that today tastes of exile
and that one day the sun will shine
like the socialist Homeland.

In the streets will be preached
the gospel of liberation,
while in the countryside
children grow like kernels of corn.

---

* compañero/a: Has no good equivalent in English, sometimes translated as "comrade," used in leftist or revolutionary situations to indicate social equality as opposed to social deference. Here, it is gendered female.

Se cantarán los himnos,
quedará atrás el dialecto de la melancolía.
Se olvidarán los dioses rindiendo culto al humano,
mujeres y hombres
haremos el amor los jueves y domingos,
religiosamente,
como conejos desnudos en los prados de Palmerola.

Amiga, sé
que no estarás conmigo
que no seré la llovizna que madure tus frutos
que no caminarás de mi mano por ese puente colgante,
ni ese río dará un paisaje
para el canto nuestro.
Sin embargo, prometo
que el triunfo del maíz y el pan se expandirá contigo
que te alzaré como a mi bandera,
tatuado estará tu influjo
en la sangre
de mil poemas heridos
por sagaces dictaduras,
rotos en los charcos de las bocacalles
y en los abrazos húmedos
por las chispeantes estrellas de un cielo sin *smog*.

Como un ejército hinchado de alegría
caminaremos
sobre espejos que proyecten la luz y la reflejen,
cuando muera la mentira, la traición, el mito,
y renazcan los imprescindibles,
en el instinto que nos unió
bajo tu afán,
mi guerrillera.

Con o sin sol, te pensaremos,
llevará el aire a tu puerta
el gorjeo de mi boca en su llamado,
y sé, compañera,
que de un futuro sueño seremos abono,

Hymns will be sung,
the dialect of melancholy will be abandoned.
Worshipping humans, gods will be forgotten
we women and men
will make love on Thursdays and Sundays,
religiously,
like naked rabbits in the field of Palmerola.

Girlfriend, I know
that you will not be with me
that I will not be the shower that matures your fruits
that you'll not walk hand-in-hand with me over that hanging bridge,
nor will that river provide a landscape
for our song.
However, I promise
that the triumph of the corn and bread will grow with you
that I will raise you like my flag,
your influence tattooed
in the blood
of a thousand poems wounded
by crafty dictatorships,
broken in the puddles at street corners
and in the moist embraces
by the shimmering stars of a sky without smog.

Like an army swollen with joy
we will walk
over mirrors that project light and reflect it,
when the lie, the betrayal, the myth die,
and the essentials are reborn,
in the instinct that joined us
at your insistence,
my guerrilla woman.

With or without sun, we will think of you,
the air will carry to your door
the trilling of my mouth in its call,
and I know, *compañera*,
that we will be food for a future dream,

que llegará el amor con su eterno reino
horadando sobre el delito y la porfía
y germinará la semilla de la esperanza
en la explosión de un universo virgen
renovado en la tierra
que, para entonces,
nos cubra.

that love will arrive with its eternal reign
piercing through offense and obstinacy
and the seed of hope will germinate
in the explosion of a virgin universe
renewed on the earth
that, by then,
will cover us.


*[Translations by María Roof]*

## HEIDY BARAHONA ALACHÁN (HEIDY ALACHÁN)
### (San Pedro Sula, 1992)

**Me dolés país**

Hoy me dolés país.
Me duele mi gente
esas criaturas
de ojos extraviados
en los pasillos
de un hospital
inhalando a cada minuto
desesperanza.
Los rostros de los niños
con la inocencia robada
en una esquina, en una calle.
Me duele la mujer
con cinco hijos
lavando ajeno
y el plato de frijoles
sin sal que a veces
hay en su mesa.
Me duelen
el conocimiento
la educación
que el niño en la montaña
o en el bordo
jamás recibirá.
Me dolés país
me dolés.

## HEIDY BARAHONA ALACHÁN (HEIDY ALACHÁN)

Elementary school teacher. Student of Juridical and Social Sciences at the National Autonomous University UNAH-Valle de Sula and of Music at the Allegro School of Music, specializing in Violin and Piano. Militant in the National Popular Resistance Front (FNRP) and the Feminist Movement of Honduras, through the Network of Young Women from Cortés. Activist in the Higher Education student movement.

**You Pain Me, Country**

Today, you pain me, country.
My people pain me
those children
with wild eyes
in hospital
corridors
each minute inhaling
desperation.
The faces of children
with their innocence stolen
on the corner, on the street.
The woman pains me
with her five children
washing for others
and the plate of beans
with no salt that sometimes
is on her table.
I am pained by
the knowledge
the education
that the child in the mountain
or in the slum
will never receive.
You pain me, country
you pain me.

## Lo invoqué

Lo invoqué,
dentro de esas paredes
arquitectónicas, de época colonial

entre las pinturas que
adornan la vista frontal
y en el rostro de quien
dicen que es él
rodeado de ángeles

lo busqué entre San Mateo,
San Marcos,
y no sé quiénes más,
en el discurso del Padre
que hablaba
como si no supiera a
quién estaba describiendo.

Me di cuenta
que estaba equivocada
Él no estaba ahí,
estaba afuera
en medio del grito de un pueblo
resistiendo la miseria
la injusticia de un sistema inhumano
condenando la violencia
y la sangre de aquellos
y aquellas caídos en lucha.

En los que no entienden
cuando les hablan de rojo o azul
si no de hambre,
necesidad y miseria
cargando penas y angustias
quienes el sol quema su espalda
y el sudor juega a
rodar por su cuerpo
para poder llevar un poco
de pan a su boca cada día.

**I Invoked Him**

I invoked him
within those walls,
architecture from the colonial period

among the paintings that
adorn the front view
and in the face of the one
they say is he
surrounded by angels

I sought him between Saint Matthew,
Saint Mark,
and I don't know who else,
in the words of the Priest
who spoke
as if he didn't know
whom he was describing

I realized
I was wrong
He was not there,
he was outside
in the midst of the shout of a people
resisting the misery
the injustice of an inhuman system
condemning the violence
and the blood of those men
and women fallen in battle.

Among those who don't understand
when they hear talk about red or blue*
but just about hunger,
need and misery
bearing suffering and anxieties
while the sun burns their back
and sweat continues to
roll down their bodies
to be able to take a little
bread to their mouths each day.

---

* Colors of flags of the traditional political parties: Liberal Party (red) and National Party (blue).

**Soy Mujer**

      Soy mujer
con el pensamiento
vistiendo mi piel.
      No me conformo
con las mentiras
que los hombres y otros tantos
escribieron sobre mí
aún sin conocerme
porque quisieron guardar mis palabras
tras el silencio impuesto.
      Soy mujer
con ojos nuevos
que sabe que el mundo
continúa detrás de la cortina.
      Soy la que piensa
sin miedo
porque tengo voz
en las manos y en mis ojos
y porque cada parte de mi cuerpo
grita mis verdades.
      Mis ideas sostienen mi frente
y ahora puedo ver con mirada firme
el camino.
      Mis palabras ya no hablan
de oficios menores
si no del deber y la necesidad
de transformar el mundo.
      Sí, soy mujer
y no solo existo
también pienso.

**I Am Woman**

       I am woman
with thought
clothing my skin.
       I don't accept
the lies
men and many others
wrote about me
even without knowing me
because they wanted to hide my words
behind imposed silence.
       I am woman
with new eyes
who knows that the world
continues behind the curtain.
       I am the one who thinks
without fear
because I have a voice
in my hands and my eyes
and because each part of my body
screams out my truths.
       My ideas sustain my brow
and now I can see with a firm gaze
the path.
       My words no longer speak
of lesser chores
but of duty and the need
to transform the world.
       Yes, I am woman
and I don't just exist
I also think.

*[Translations by María Roof]*

## GILDA BATISTA
### (Honduras, 1964)

**Ustedes**

A ustedes los conozco bien
ustedes que piensan que el pueblo es una marioneta
ustedes saben lo que yo sé
ustedes quieren hacer lo mismo
someter al pueblo
tenerlo vagando en la miseria
en la impotencia.
Ustedes que son desalmados
unos inseguros.
Ustedes
solo son un puño
de narcisistas.

Ustedes que creen que el pueblo es una pestilencia
ustedes lo que son, son una porqueriza.
Truena el cielo
y se corre la voz
que ustedes son un asco
de Dios.

Truena el cielo y se corre la voz
y el agua sigue chorreando.
Truena y se corre la voz

**GILDA BATISTA**

Painter, sculptor, feminist, writer. Member of National Association of Honduran Women Writers (ANDEH) and of the Art Protest Movement—Psychotic, Brutal/Insane Art and/or Street Art. Human Rights defender. Inspired by the continuous struggle of human beings, especially those of her country, who live submerged in poverty, the cause of great mental and physical anguish. Antipoverty activist who seeks mental, social, and economic balance. Her paintings and sculptures invoke artistic themes from the ancient Mayans and colors utilized by Afro-Hondurans. Owner of g. Batista Art Gallery.

**You People**

I know you well
you who think that the people are a puppet
you know what I know
that you want to do the same
subjugate the people
have them wallowing in misery
in impotence.
You who are soulless
and insecure.
You people
are just a handful
of narcissists.

You who believe that the people are a pestilence
what you are is a herd of swine.
The sky thunders
and the rumor flies
that you are disgusting
to God.

The sky thunders and the rumor flies
and water keeps gushing.
It thunders and the rumor flies

que el dolor sigue
sigue el dolor por el amor

Pienso en esa serpiente
en esa cría,
como intuyo
porque soy serpiente
una vieja serpiente
que el olfato
no se esconde.

Amo.
Amo lo que huelo
lo que me seduce.

Esta vez se jodieron
golpistas de mierda.

*(g. Batista 05 junio 2012)*

that pain continues
pain for love continues.

I think of that serpent
of that brood,
as I intuit
because I am a serpent
an old serpent
who doesn't hide
her sense of smell.

I love.
I love what I smell
what seduces me.

This time you screwed yourselves
you worthless *golpistas*.

    *(g. Batista June 5, 2012)*

**Solo Quiero Tres**

No quiero ver árboles de Navidad
ni tampoco a Santa en su trineo
lo que quiero son tres vergazos de guaro
y tres puros de marihuana
y sentarme frente al mar
para invocar al dios de la guerra
y pedirle que envíe su ira
contra el sistema neoliberal.

Dicen ser cristianos
intercambian obsequios para Noche Buena
Rolex dice la etiqueta.
Quiero tres puros de marihuana
y tres vergazos de guaro
para invocar al diablo
para que se lleve al puto infierno
a los malditos malhechores
al presidente de la Puta República
al presidente del Congreso Sin Vergüenza Nacional
y al presidente de la Corte Suprema de Injusticia.

Quiero tres puros de marihuana
y tres vergazos bajo el sol
y pedirle a la Luna
que ilumine el camino
de los pobres, para que levanten
su ira contra el sistema neoliberal.

*(g. Batista 01 de diciembre 2012)*

## I Just Want Three

I don't want to see Christmas trees
or Santa in his sleigh
I just want three slugs of *guaro**
and three marijuana joints
and sit by the sea
invoke the god of war
and ask him to send his ire
against the neoliberal system.

They say they are Christians
they exchange gifts on Christmas Eve
Rolex the label says.
I want three marijuana joints
and three slugs of *guaro*
to invoke the devil
so he can take to deepest hell
the damned criminals
the president of the Whoring Republic
the president of the National No Shame Congress
and the president of the Supreme Court of Injustice.

I want three marijuana joints
and three slugs under the sun
and to ask the Moon
to light the way
for the poor, so they can raise
their wrath against the neoliberal system.

(g. Batista December 1, 2012)

---

* *guaro:* A sweet, clear, alcoholic liquor distilled from sugar cane juices.

## AMANECIÓ EN HONDURAS

Amaneció en Honduras:
crímenes por doquier,
políticos transando,
familias mandando,
la Corte y el Congreso trampeando;
y los pobres hambreando.

Amaneció en Honduras:
inundada de pobreza,
mojada de corrupción,
ahogada en la impunidad,
zambullida en deuda.

Amaneció en Honduras:
tierra de intelectuales sin intelecto,
suelo de bestias políticas,
terruño de oportunistas,
cielo de los académicos corruptos,
infierno de los pobres.

Amaneció en Honduras:
hincada,
sin la esperanza de amanecer,
sin el consuelo del anochecer,
calada en miseria,
entregada por el Lobo,
devorada por el Dictador,
sumida en tristeza.

*(g. Batista 02 Julio de 2013)*

## DAY DAWNED IN HONDURAS

Day dawned in Honduras:
crimes everywhere
politicians swindling,
families ruling,
the Court and Congress playing tricks;
and poor people hungering.

Day dawned in Honduras:
flooded with poverty,
drenched in corruption,
drowned in impunity,
plunged into debt.

Day dawned in Honduras:
land of intellectuals without intellect,
ground of political beasts,
homeland of opportunists,
heaven of corrupt academics,
hell of the poor.

Day dawned in Honduras:
on its knees,
without dawn's hope,
without night's consolation,
dripping in misery,
surrendered by the Lobo wolf,
devoured by the Dictator,
immersed in sadness.

    *(g. Batista July 2, 2013)*

*[Translations by María Roof]*

# REBECA BECERRA LANZA
(Tegucigalpa, 1969)

## REFUNDACIÓN

*Para Erick Martínez Ávila*
*Asesinado*

Siguen sonando las campanas de la muerte. Su desconsolada resonancia consterna el alma. Una y otra vez nos abren a los caminos de la sangre y nos empujan hacia sus siniestras veredas. Nos reconocemos en cada uno de los cuerpos que día a día son encontrados como solitarios desechos esperando el olor de nuestras flores.
   Los ángeles que guardan nuestras humildes camas se han convertido en demonios de la conciencia. La justicia, galope de los Jinetes de la Apocalipsis se pierde en la espesura de un oscuro bosque.
   Hay palabras que no pueden llegar a las bocas de los que cimientan la muerte porque les aterroriza su vaho pestilente. La carencia los ha impedido, solamente ven por las rendijas de las foscas alcantarillas y no se dan cuenta que aran la tierra equivocada.
   Nosotros estamos en el lado correcto del río, aquí es donde

**REBECA BECERRA LANZA**

Degree in Letters from the National Autonomous University (UNAH). Cofounder of the poetry workshop Casa Tomada (1992); cofounder of Ixbalam Editores (2000) and the journal *Ixbalam*. Awarded the "Hugo Lindo" Central American Poetry Prize, San Salvador, El Salvador (1992). Finalist in numerous national literary contests. Author of two books of poetry: *Sobre las mismas piedras* (On the Same Stones, 2004) and *Las palabras del aire* (Words of the Air, 2006). Consultant in socioanthropology. Former General Director of Books and Documents, Secretariat of Culture, Arts and Sports. The Inter-American Court of Human Rights granted her and her two daughters protective measures, since she was the target of death threats and illegal detention because of her position against the 2009 coup d'état.

**REFOUNDATION**
   *To Erick Martínez Ávila*
   *Murdered*

The bells of death still toll. Their inconsolable resonance troubles the soul. Once and again they open onto roads of blood and push us toward their sinister paths. We recognize ourselves in each one of the corpses that day after day are found as lonely discards awaiting the fragrance of our flowers.

Angels that guard our humble beds have become demons of conscience. Justice, the gallop of the Horsemen of the Apocalypse, is lost in the thickness of a dark forest.

Some words cannot come into the mouths of those who proclaim death, because they are terrified of their pestilent breath. Absence has hampered them; they see only through cracks in dank sewers and do not realize that they plow the wrong land.

We are on the right side of the river; here, the light comes

llega la luz y se divierte en sus colores. Por aquí corre el agua y su susurro que arrulla la esperanza. Aquí está la sombra blanca de la vida, el viento que sopla en nuestras manos las banderas que ya no pueden arrebatarnos. La lluvia que nos cuenta en cada gota la historia de nuestra carne de maíz y nuestros dedos de obsidiana.

Aquí construiremos el nuevo Popol Nah, con la saliva de la jícara de Hun Hunahpu y la espuma blanca de Patakako fijaremos cada piedra. Pata Cher-Kama elaborará las hamacas que sosegarán nuestro cansancio. Toman Pones y Popawai levantarán del día la sangre de la noche y nos librarán del tiempo que teje la muerte.

Habrá principio. Reinarán los colores en las plumas de los pájaros y las hojas del pasto se trenzarán con el nuevo viento.

*8 mayo 2012*

and plays with its colors. Water runs here, and its murmur whispers to hope. Here is the white shadow of life, the wind that waves the flags in our hands that can no longer be wrenched from us. The rain that narrates with each drop the history of our corn flesh and obsidian fingers.

Here we will build the new Popol Nah; with saliva from the bowl of Hun Hunahpu and the white foam of Patakako we will place each stone. Pata Cher-Kama will make the hammocks that will calm our fatigue. Toman Pones and Popawai will lift from the day the blood of night and will free us from the time that death weaves.

There will be a beginning. Colors will reign in the feathers of birds and the leaves of grass will braid together with the new wind.

*May 8, 2012*

*[Translation by Andrea Gaytán Cuesta]*

## NOEMÍ BORJAS RODRÍGUEZ
(Guaimaca, Francisco Morazán, 1966)

**Un golpe a la esperanza**

Se confundieron los ruidos:
de aviones verdes,
sollozos
de una esperanza que moría;
la asfixiaban las bombas
que al unísono estallaban.

Fue tanto el ruido
que despertó mi memoria,
mi corazón,
mis ansias de justicia,
de revolución.

*Julio 10, 2009*

## NOEMÍ BORJAS RODRÍGUEZ

University degree in Foreign Languages, National Autonomous University (UNAH). Studies in International Relations and Social Demography. English professor at UNAH.


## A Coup's Blow to Hope

The sounds came all at once:
roars from green planes,
sobs
of a dying hope;
smothered by the bombs
exploding simultaneously.

The noise was so loud
it awakened my memory,
my heart,
my longing for justice,
for revolution.

*July 10, 2009*

**Bienvenida a un líder**

Hasta aquí llegó el odio
se recibió con alfombras
tejidas de rojo.
Secretos hilos que tejían
un sueño honroso
corrían tímidamente
por ti, mi ciudad humillada.
Se fueron uniendo con otros
volviéndose fuertes
impregnando el suelo hasta lo infinito
dejando células inertes
que un día brotarán
con luz, humanidad, libertad.

*Tegucigalpa, Sept. 22, 09*
*(En toque de queda ordenado por Micheletti)*

## Welcome to a Leader

Hatred came here
and was received on carpets
woven of red.
Secret threads weaving
an honorable dream
ran timidly
through you, my humiliated city.
They began to join others
becoming strong
seeding the land infinitely
with quiet cells
that one day will burst into flowers
of light, humanity, liberty.

*Tegucigalpa. Sept 22, 2009*
*(During the curfew ordered by Interim President Roberto Micheletti on this date)*


*[Translations by Jonathan Arries]*

## XIOMARA BU
## (Tegucigalpa, 1956)

**MIEDO**

Sabía
que al pronunciar
la palabra
justicia
resurgiría
la luz de las velas.
Cuánto miedo
tenemos
de vivir
en nuestra casa
ungiendo
los dolores.
La lucha
por la vida
no es fácil
cuando la bota aprieta
y el fusil extermina
la fuerza de la vida.
Nos disfrazamos
día a día
y vestimos el andamiaje

## XIOMARA BU

Philosophy professor at the National Autonomous University (UNAH), with degrees in Philosophy from the University of Costa Rica and in Juridical Sciences from the UNAH, and graduate studies in Philosophy of Science at the Catholic University of America (Washington, DC). Defender of the human rights of people HIV-positive and living with AIDS and coordinator of the National Forum on AIDS. Her first book of poems, *Fuego en el silencio* (Fire in Silence, 1993), won the 1992 poetry contest held by the UNAH Association of Professors in the University Course of General Studies (UNAH-APECUEG). Published essay: *Dominio y polarización de los géneros* (Domination and Polarization of Genders, 1994). These poems are from her unpublished collection, *Diálogo con las sombras* (Dialogue with Shadows).

## FEAR

I knew
that when I pronounced
the word
justice
the light of candles
would revive.
What fear
we feel
to live
in our home
salving
our pains.
The struggle
for life
is not easy
when the boot squashes
and the rifle terminates
the life force.
We dress in costumes
day by day
and don the scaffolding

de los mejores circos
que no exhiben la cara
de la melancolía.
El grito queda atrapado
sólo el río fluye
mientras desvanece
el pretendido escenario
que teje en fisuras
banderas libertarias
el lobo asolapado
brinda tributos
saca sus garras
y coloca en costales
cuerpos
descuartizados.

of the best circuses
that don't show the face
of melancholy.
The scream gets stuck
only the river flows
while the supposed stage
disappears
that weaves fissures into
liberty flags
the Lobo wolf dressed up
toasts tributes
bears his claws
and puts in sacks
bodies
dismembered.

**Tensión**

Entre el deseo y la razón
una vida vivida sin justicia.
Al borde de la irracionalidad
ha llegado la hora
de afirmar la existencia
dejando los velos de la noche
en las pupilas del buitre.
Abandonemos
el miedo al Yo auténtico
desafiante de miserias.
Solo los topos tienen temor
de liberar al esclavo
vivimos una lluvia de sombras
en la insondable eternidad.

**Tension**

Between desire and reason
a life lived without justice.
On the verge of irrationality
the time has come
to affirm existence
leaving the veils of night
in the pupils of the vulture.
Let's abandon
fear of the authentic "I"
defiant of miseries.
Only moles are afraid
to liberate the slave
we live in a rain of shadows
in endless eternity.

**MI PATRIA**

Mi patria juega
a los cautiverios día a día
no se dan cuenta
nos conquistaron
con espejitos plásticos.
Bebieron hasta saciar su sed.
Llegó la independencia
con eternas cadenas
se llama dependencia.
Mi patria tiene las venas abiertas
y sangra cada noche.
Aquí no repican las campanas.

*Honduras-Junio 2009*

**MY COUNTRY**

My country plays
at captivities each day
they don't realize
they conquered us
with little plastic mirrors.
They drank until sating their thirst.
Independence came
with eternal chains
called dependence.
My country has its veins open
and bleeds every night.
Here, no bells chime.

    *Honduras, June 2009*


[*Translations by María Roof*]

## XIOMARA CACHO CABALLERO
### (Bay Islands, Roatán, 1968)

**Desiguales**

      Nací en un país de ciudadanía
famélica, necesitada y miserable
violenta, descalza, muerta de hambre
y de humanidad desigual
      Donde abundan varones acumuladores
de bienes y capitales; patria que produce aniquilados
en donde el patrimonio sirve
para los fines de las oligarquías
      En donde los seres abandonan la convicción
y se burlan de la esperanza, país en donde se esparce
el cinismo y la desconfianza;
se soslayan las oportunidades a la sombra
de ágapes y fiestas excluyentes
      Mi país es de sociedad injusta, capitalista y de estructuras
inmorales
de académicos e intelectuales miserables
y cada vez más carentes de dignidad,
que tienen como virtud no hacer el bien a los demás
sino que desplegar marginación, exclusión y miseria.

# XIOMARA CACHO CABALLERO

Originally from the first Garífuna community in Honduras, Punta Gorda, Roatán, Bay Islands. Master's in Human Rights Education and degree in English from the Francisco Morazán National Pedagogical University (UPNFM); diploma in Special Education, Harris-Stowe State University, St. Louis, Missouri. First place in Essay, National Literary Contest, 2010; "Juan Manuel Posse Gold Laurel Award," from the Sociedad Femenina de Letras Grupo Ideas (Ideas Group, Women's Society of Letters). Speaker of Garífuna, English and Spanish. Greatest Honduran figure in Afro-descended literature. Books: *Tumálali Nanigi/ La voz del corazón/ The Voice of the Heart* (1998); *Arena húmeda* (Wet Sand); *Wafien tuma lisisiran/ Wafien y sus maracas/ Wafien and His Rattles* (2000); *Bungiü Wuriti/ Dios negro/ Black Jesus* (2003); *Poesía, cantos, ceremonias y vestimenta de la cultura garífuna* (Poetry, Songs, Ceremonies and Dress of Garífuna Culture); *Isubuse* (Garífuna poetry); *Ruguma* (novel); and others.

## Unequals

     I was born in a country whose citizens are
starving, needy and miserable
violent, barefoot, dying of hunger
and of unequal humanity
     Where men abound who accumulate
goods and capital; a country that produces crushed people
where the national patrimony serves
the oligarchies' purposes
     Where beings abandon conviction
and make fun of hope; country where
cynicism and distrust are scattered about;
opportunities bypassed in the shadow
of exclusive banquets and parties
     My country is an unjust, capitalist society of immoral structures
of miserable academics and intellectuals
lacking more and more dignity,
who think it a virtue not to do good unto others
but to deploy marginalization, exclusion and misery.

## Licencia para delinquir

¿Por qué causan nerviosismo en tu espíritu, estas palabras?
Y las voces de la ciudadanía inquieta inquiriendo
solidaridad con su pueblo que está siendo
vilmente masacrado
¡Despierta!
¿O es que estás acostumbrado a la penumbra y al pánico?
¿O es que acaso te ofende la luz?
¡Mira a tu pueblo empobrecido! Sufriendo en carne propia
la privación de sus derechos
Ven y busca interpretar el consagrado sistema de
privilegios
que oculta en varias piezas articuladas la dominación;
voracidad predatoria e ideológica perniciosa
con licencia para delinquir
Despierta para restablecer el imperio de la ley
los rostros ajados, los ojos rojizos e inflamados, cuerpos
sudorosos, con taquicardia y agitadas respiraciones,
causado por el caos e inestabilidad
¡Allí viene! ¡Allí viene! El pueblo atormentado,
que ha sufrido tanto y que eleva su lamento,
para que desaparezca la rancia oligarquía
que día a día persiste en seguir en la cima,
sin importar las desigualdades e injusticias

## License to Commit Crime

      Why do these words make your spirit nervous?
And the voices of the restless public demanding
solidarity with its people who are being
vilely massacred
Wake up!
      Or are you accustomed to darkness and panic?
Or perhaps light offends you?
Look at your impoverished people! Suffering in their bodies
the loss of their rights
      Come and try to explain the sacred system of privileges
that hides domination in its many jointed parts;
predatory greed and harmful ideology
with a license to commit crime
      Wake up to re-establish the rule of law
aged faces, bloodshot, swollen eyes, sweaty
bodies, with tachycardia and shortness of breath,
caused by chaos and instability
      Here they come! Here they come! The tortured people,
who have suffered so much raising their cry
to make the rancid oligarchy disappear
that day after day persists in remaining at the top
with no concern for inequalities and injustices

**Pide a gritos el castigo**

    De manera infame despliegan ideologías manipuladoras
sumisión e imposición de razones
disfrazadas en democracia clasista y autoritaria
sin importar el sufrimiento de la población
    Acostumbrados a
estrangular los sueños
disminuir la libertad y la aspiración
para satisfacer ambiciones personales
    Pide a gritos el castigo,
pide a gritos, Justicia que aplique las leyes
sistema contencioso eficiente
que consolide de manera sustantiva la democracia
    Una institucionalidad eficaz que modifique
la decadencia moral
coincidente con el pecado
garante de terminar con la corrupción.

## Demand Punishment Screaming

      They despicably deploy manipulative ideologies,
submissiveness and the imposition of reasons
disguised in classist and authoritarian democracy
with no regard for the suffering of the people
      Accustomed to
strangling dreams,
diminishing liberty and aspiration
in order to satisfy personal ambitions
      Demand punishment screaming,
demand screaming that Justice enforce the law
in a system of efficient litigation
that substantively consolidates democracy
      An effective institutionality that changes
the moral decline
coincident with sin
and guarantees an end to corruption.


*[Translations by Mesi Walton]*

## DORA ESPERANZA CÁLIX MOLINA
### (Juticalpa, Olancho, 1944)

**Porque me asiste la razón**

Después de tanta iniquidad
me obligo patria
a caminar contigo.
María y Sebastián
salidos del olvido,
la esperanza
que tantos siglos de dolor
llevan ungida,
enarbolaron ayer.
He aprendido,
que como ellos
me asiste la razón.
A la utopía
se llega
por distintos senderos,
que no hay muros de tanques
ni corazas militares
ni sátrapas,
ni bombas lacrimógenas
que apaguen el clamor
de los ungidos.
Los pueblos irredentos
no conocen el miedo;
andan a tientas
cuando el invierno es fuerte,

## DORA ESPERANZA CÁLIX MOLINA

Retired professor of Elementary Education, field which stimulated her interest in literature. Degree in Educational Sciences and a specialist in Pre-school Education, where she affirmed her social commitment. Two published collections: *Del recuerdo y otros haceres* (On Memory and Other Activities, 1998); *El otro lado de la soledad* (The Other Side of Solitude, 2007). In preparation, *Después del mediodía* (After Noon).

### Because Reason Is on My Side

After so much iniquity
I force myself, homeland,
to walk with you.
María and Sebastián,
rising out of oblivion,
the hope
for so many centuries of pain
borne anointed,
they hoisted yesterday.
I have learned,
that, like for them,
reason is on my side.
You get to utopia
by different paths,
no walls of tanks
nor military shields
nor usurpers,
nor teargas bombs
can silence the clamor
of those anointed.
Unredeemed peoples
know no fear;
they walk cautiously
when winter is fierce,

pero nunca se parten
a la primera brisa;
Obed se fue tal vez
para alumbrar la aurora,
pero ni aquel lucero
ni Róger ni Magdiel
tenían prisa;
el dictador cortó su piel,
los hizo misa
hoy son plegaria
y oración,
consigna y grito redentor,
porque en verdad no han muerto.
Cómo desangran los pueblos
detrás de sus ideales;
cómo riegan ideales
los pueblos con su sangre;
por eso,
después de tanta iniquidad
me obligo, patria
a caminar contigo.

*Agosto 2009*

but they never move on
with the first wind;
Obed left perhaps
to light up the dawn,
but neither that bright star
nor Róger nor Magdiel
were in a hurry;
the dictator sliced their skin,
made them into a church mass
today they are supplication
and prayer,
watchword and redemptive battle cry,
because they did not really die.
How the peoples bleed
for their ideals;
how the peoples irrigate ideals
with their blood;
that is why,
after so much iniquity
I force myself, homeland,
to walk with you.

*August 2009*

### ¿Qué puedes ofrecerme, patria?

Tus manos talladas
en tortillas de maíz
pizque amanecido;
¿un mar seco de ilusiones
con arenas viajeras
que se hinchan al viento,
en la serenidad postrera
o bordada en versos
con el lenguaje de los paisajes
idos?
Perfiles desnudos
¡Sólo atesoras tu nombre!
Riachuelos
ilusiones mutiladas,
presos quizás
en la cansada hierba,
en la mudez de las ranas
en las apagadas luciérnagas del bosque
en el arco iris
sin colores nacarados.
Me duelen
tus intranquilas olas
vestidas con el rumor
embrujante de las errabundas
sirenas de la mar.
¿Qué puedes patria ofrecerme?
Un mundo de esperanzas
tempranas
hilvanadas con las huellas
de los matices de tu verdad.
El blanco y el azul de tu bandera,
airosa,
resplandeciendo
en una era nueva,
en una paz solemne
que musiten tus hijos:
era nueva,
Paz solemne,
Tierra de libertad.

*Junio 2009*

## What Can You Offer Me, Homeland?

Your hands molded
in corn tortillas
newborn stalks;
perhaps, a dry sea of illusions
with shifting sands
that rise with the wind,
in later serenity
or embroidered in verses
with the language of landscapes
departed?
Denuded profiles
You treasure only your name!
Streams
mutilated illusions,
captured perhaps
in the tired grass,
in the muteness of frogs
in the extinguished fireflies of the forest
in the rainbow
without pearled colors.
I am pained by
your unquiet waves
dressed in the bewitching
sound of the wandering
sirens of the sea.
What can you offer me, homeland?
A world of hopes
early ones
woven with traces
of the hues of your truth.
The white and blue of your flag,
flying high,
glowing
in a new era,
in a solemn peace
that your children could whisper:
new era,
solemn Peace
Land of freedom.

*June 2009*

**En pocas palabras**

El mundo
       Nosotros
Nosotras
       Tú
Y
       Yo
Niños locos
       Gritándole
Al hambre
       Derramada
Por el
       Suelo.

**In A Few Words**

The world
      We all
We women
      You
And
      I
Crazed kids
      Screaming
At hunger
      Shed
Over the
      Ground.

*[Translations by María Roof]*

## DORIS MELISSA CARDOZA CALDERÓN
### (Siguatepeque, Comayagua, 1966)

**Plegaria**
*Para Amanda Castro*

Para nombrarte
deberíamos estar limpias de golpes y humo
de muertas
de dolores
Para decir tu nombre en esta tu ausencia
habría que entender más
y odiar menos
esperar sabiendo que el rencor pudre todo
¡quién tuviera tu nobleza!

Esta tierra donde nos dejaste
esta matriz que nos parió a todas
se desangra
nosotras dormimos, pero sin descanso
y los asesinos no detienen su marcha
aplastando cuerpos de mujeres que, como vos, enseñaban

Amanda,
un día sólo tendremos flores y cantos para nombrarte
tortillas recién hechitas con olor a tierra dignificada
y un jardín de niñas sin miedo
Pero hoy quedate con nosotras
       no nos dejés ahora
en esta hora del mal y la esperanza.

# DORIS MELISSA CARDOZA CALDERÓN

Writer, popular educator, feminist, defender of the rights of indigenous peoples; self-defined as a "Black Lenca" (of the indigenous group) and "delusional dreamer of justice, good love and pleasures." Member of Feminists in Resistance, formed during the 2009 coup. Books: *Textos zafados* (Unhooked Texts, 2004); *13 colores de la resistencia hondureña* (Thirteen Colors of Honduran Resistance, 2011). Video: *"Resistencia en Honduras*/The Resistance in Honduras," Doris Melissa Cardoza Calderón hablando en Ljubljana (Éslovenia) sobre Resistencia popular contra golpe de estado en Honduras/... speaking in Ljubljana (Slovenia) about coup d'état and people's resistance in Honduras. January 10, 2010. VIMEO, 33 mins. http://vimeo.com/7271005.

**Prayer**
*For Amanda Castro*

    To name you
we should be free from blows and smoke
of dead women
of pains
To say your name in your absence
we should understand more
and hate less
wait while knowing that bitterness rots everything
no one was as noble as you!

This land where you left us
this womb that bore all us women
is bleeding to death
we sleep, but without resting
and murderers do not stop their march
crushing bodies of women who, like you, were teachers

Amanda,
one day we will have only flowers and songs to name you
freshly made tortillas smelling of a dignified soil
and a garden of girls without fear
But stay with us today
    don't leave us now
at this hour of evil and hope.

**Amar de golpe**

En estas noches de golpe
dormir en Tegucigalpa no es dormir
es olvidar.
El cuerpo suma sueños insanos
vigilias de miedo y rabia
largas noches de espera, de cárcel
de ruegos, fugas y rezos
En estos días de golpe
vivir en Tegucigalpa no es vivir
es andar
conciencia alerta sobre el que mira con el blanco ojo del mal
Cruzar la calle de las sospechas una y otra vez
sonreír a la compañera de al lado en las filas que surcan
    barrios.
Amar en Tegucigalpa, en estos tiempos de golpe
no es amar como antes
con nombres y apellidos
porque el corazón está en la resistencia

*agosto 2009*

## To Love All of A Sudden

During these nights of the coup
to sleep in Tegucigalpa is not to sleep
it is to forget.
The body collects insane dreams
wakefulness filled with fear and rage
long nights of waiting, of prison
of pleas, escapes and prayers
During these days of the coup
to live in Tegucigalpa is not to live
it is to walk
awareness alert to the man looking with the white eye of evil
To cross the street of suspicions time and again
to smile at the woman next to you in the rows that cross
        neighborhoods.
To love in Tegucigalpa, during these times of the coup
is not to love like before
with names and last names
because the heart is in the resistance

*August 2009*

**Tengo una hija en la mente**

Tengo una hija en la mente
y un duelo que me llena el vientre de nada
Perdí amigas
niños-hombres que no conocí
Me quitaron los golpistas la vida que no había venido
y me dieron un tropel de mujeres indignadas
con ellas canto en silencio
conspiro en las miradas
Por ellas resisto
al aliento de la palabra envenenada
al abismo de la guerra que nos llama

# I Have a Daughter in My Mind

I have a daughter in my mind
and a mourning that fills my womb with nothing
I lost girlfriends
boys-men I didn't know
The *golpistas* took from me a life that was yet to come
and gave me a crowd of angered women
with them I sing in silence
I conspire in their looks
For them I resist
the breath of the poisoned word
the abyss of the war that calls us


*[Translations by Stephanie Saunders]*

# AMANDA CASTRO
(Tegucigalpa, 1962-2010)

**Sirven las palabras...**

De qué sirven/ éstas mis estúpidas palabras/ que murmuran desde la oquedad/ Profunda/ de mi Ser/ para romper/ en mil sonidos el silencio/ De qué sirven/ escalofríos estremecimientos/ que cabalgan las espinas/ recordándonos/ la humanidad/ de qué sirve pasarse el día entero escaneando información/ verificándola/ para ponerla en un blog/ que sólo leerán apenas 30 personas/ en todo el mundo/ ¿de qué sirve?/ me pregunto/

Y aparecen en mis manos/ los milagros de los días/ alargándonos la vida/ franqueando condenas a muerte/ entrelazándome/ con otras/otros/ que como yo/ también se preguntan para qué sirven sus palabras/ y de pronto/ cae el veinte/ de la mismísima manera que cae una gota de lluvia en la

# AMANDA CASTRO

Ph.D., Sociolinguistics, University of Pittsburgh. Resident in U.S. after 1985. University professor and promoter of Central American literature and art. Defender of human rights of women, especially in the maquila shops. Founder of Ixbalam press and journal. First Poetry Prize, 56th Juegos Florales for Mexico, Central America and the Caribbean, 1993. Golden Laurel Leaf Medal, awarded by the government of President Manuel Zelaya, 2008. She suffered lung problems, and her health deteriorated after the 2009 coup, which she vehemently opposed. She died on March 18, 2010. Published poetry collections include: *Poemas de amor propio y de propio amor* (Poems of Self-Love and of Love Itself, 1993); *Celebración de Mujeres* (Celebration of Women, 1996); *Onironautas* (Dreamnauts, 2001); *Quizás la sangre* (Perhaps the Blood, 2001); *La otra cara del sol* (The Other Face of the Sun, 2001); *Una vez un barco* (Once A Boat, 2001); *El paso de la muerte* (The Passing of Death, 2006); *Desnuda y sin tregua* (Naked and Restless, 2010 posthumously). The two poems included here were discovered by researching files, networks and among the poet's friends. They are published for the first time, post mortem, with the approval of Amanda Castro's wife and are reproduced in the original format.

**Words Are Good For...**

What good are/ these stupid words of mine/ that murmur from the Profound/ void/ of my Being/ to break/ the silence into a thousand sounds/ What good are/ chills tremblings/ that ride the spine/ reminding us of/ humanity/ what good is spending the whole day scanning information/ checking it/ to put in a blog/ that maybe only 30 people will read/ in the whole world/ what good is it?/ I wonder/

And appearing in my hands/ the miracles of days/ lengthening our lives/ commuting death sentences/ linking me/ to other women/ men/ who like me/ also wonder what their words are good for / and suddenly/ the twentieth falls/ just like a drop of rain falls in the Sea/ to join with it and

Mar/ para poblarla y completarse/ perdiéndose en el anonimato/ de una maza gigantesca que se mueve/ y que se agranda con cada ser/ con cada ínfimo elemento/ que constituye esto que llamamos vida/ con cada voz/s/

Sirven/ para calmar la sed/ y engendrar esa otra justicia/ que se añora y que se busca/ esa de saberse esencialmente buena/ limpia y clara/ igual que la poesía/ de saber que en efecto las palabras SON la vida/ que también/ al final/ nos acompaña el Verbo/

Sirven/ para calmar el dolor/ ése que Hondo nos destrozaba el alma/ cuando nombrarlo no podíamos/ ahora que lo conocemos/ y le hemos visto el rostro/ y hemos despertado/ no podemos nosotras/ nosotros/ más que repudiarlo/ Sanarnos los golpes/ curar las heridas/ limpiar nuestra sangre/ cantar y bailar/ gozando/ este cambio de era/ que certero llega hasta las profecías/

Sirven/ para volver al sol/ a la luna/ y no necesariamente 40 años después/ sirven para volver/ a caminar/ llevando en alto/ "el féretro de una estrella"/ y un estandarte de paz/ teñido de sangre/ y no blanco como aquel falso/

Sirven las palabras/ para re/conocernos/ e identi/ficarnos/ y sabernos/ hermanos y hermanas/ kompas en lucha/ —porque el sentarse en silencio/ también es lucha—/ y ver cómo nos vamos hallando/ en las redes que ni siquiera existen/

Sirven las palabras para desatar/ vendavales/ ventiscas/ polen y semen/ y engendrar los vuelos/ chamana/es en punto/ listos los rituales quemado el incienso/ logros alcanzados/ discursos apropiados/ proyectos concluidos/ —cooperación/ interna—/

complete itself/ losing itself in the anonymity/ of a gigantic club that moves/ and grows larger with each being/ with each infinitesimal element/ that constitutes this that we call life/ with each voice/s/

They are good/ for calming thirst/ and engendering that other justice/ that is longed for and sought/ the one by which you know you are essentially a good/ clean and clear woman/ just like poetry/ you know that in effect words ARE life/ and also/ in the end/ that the Word accompanies us/

They are good/ for calming pain/ the one that was Deeply destroying our soul/ when we couldn't name it/ now that we know it/ and we have seen its face/ and we have awakened/ we women cannot/ or men either/ do anything but condemn it/ Heal our blows/ cure our wounds/ clean our blood/ sing and dance/ enjoying/ this change of era/ that will surely last 'til the prophecies/

They are good/ for returning to the sun/ to the moon/ and not necessarily 40 years later/ they are good for/ walking again/ carrying on high/ "the coffin of a star"/ and a standard of peace/ stained with blood/ and not white like the false one/

Words are good/ for re/knowing and recognizing ourselves/ and identi/fying ourselves/ and knowing ourselves to be/ brothers and sisters/ *kompas** in the struggle/ –because sitting in silence/ is also struggle–/ and see how we are finding each other / in networks that don't even exist

Words are good for unleashing/ windstorms/ gales/ pollen and semen/ and engendering shaman flights on time/ the rituals ready incense burned/ successes achieved/ appropriate speeches/ projects concluded/–internal cooperation–/

---

* "kompas," abbreviation of "compañeros," meaning colleagues, companions, like-minded people.

Sirven/ para ampliar el mundo/ para ver las fuentes/ y escuchar los ecos/ y contar/ los pasos que marchan/ de prisa/ mientras cruzan las balas/ el fondo sagrado/ y el pálido Azul/

Sirven las palabras/ para salvarnos/ de esta muerte certera/ que semeja el olvido/ en las noches frías y solas/ sentadas con hambre/ entre las montañas/ soñando tu amor/

Sirven/ las palabras/ sirven/ apenas para mencionar la Hondura/ que yace/ herida y sangrienta/ esperando/ esperándote a vos/

*(amanda castro/ comayagüela/ honduras/ 28 de julio del 2009/ un mes en resistencia/)*

They are good/ for broadening the world/ to see the sources/ and listen to the echoes/ and count/ the steps that march/ quickly/ while shots are fired/ the sacred backdrop/ and the pale Blue/

Words are good/ for saving us/ from this certain death/ that is like oblivion/ on cold and lonely nights/ sitting with hunger/ in the mountains/ dreaming your love/

Words/ are good/ are good/ barely for mentioning the Hondura/ that lies/ wounded and bloody/ waiting/ waiting for you/

>   *(amanda castro/comayagüela/ honduras/ July 28, 2009/ one month in resistance/)*

**Que pasen todas las mujeres**

Que pasen todas las mujeres que se han visto obligadas a trabajar en el campo/ y en las maquilas/ y sobreviven la violencia del acoso sexual en el trabajo/ y mutilan sus cuerpos/ produciendo/ millares de prendas/ tejidas con agujas de sangre/ para poder darle a sus hija/os una vida más digna/ mujeres que pierden su cuerpo/ doce horas de pie/ en movimientos forzados/ anti/naturales/ para que puedan/ gringos/koreanos/ europeos/ y demás/ hartarse manjares en las costas de marfil/ y en casa blanca/

**Let All the Women Pass**

Let all the women pass who have been forced to work in the fields/ in the maquilas/ and who endure sexual assault violence at work/ and mutilate their bodies/ producing/ thousands of pieces of clothing/ woven with needles of blood/ to be able to give their daughters/sons a more dignified life/ women who lose their bodies/ standing twelve hours / in forced movements/ anti/natural ones/ so that/ gringos/ Koreans/ Europeans/ and others can/ feast on delicacies in ivory coasts/ and in the white house/

*[Translations by María Roof]*

## YADIRA EGUIGURE
### (La Esperanza, Intibucá, 1971)

**Aquí, en esta Honduras entrañable, se escribe la historia**
*Para mi Luna que, tan pequeñita como es,*
*ya pregunta y entiende cómo duele la patria.*

En este lugar tan hondo de la América herida
corre el llanto y el sudor confundiéndose
       /sobre la marcha;
un sabor a lágrima se desliza
       /desde el cielo
lloviendo en testimonio fijo de tinta
       /sobre paredes.
Aquí se escribe la historia
con rostros de hambre, de rabia, de luto;
se escribe con brazos, con alma, con ideales,
con tinta firme, con puño claro, con paso lento,
con la ilusión de que algo mejor se gesta:
se escribe en el corazón de los mártires.

Aquí la muerte elige máscaras en rostros bravos:
Isi Murillo, Pedro Magdiel, Róger Vallejo,
Pablo Hernández...

Se manifiesta en medio de la gente, la abraza
       /suave,
mientras disimula su huesuda fisonomía.

# YADIRA EGUIGURE

Educator, poet. Degree in Letters from Francisco Morazán National Pedagogical University (UPNFM).

## Here, in This Beloved Honduras, History is Written

*For my Moon who, as tiny as she is,*
*Already inquires and understands how the nation suffers.*

In this place so deep in wounded America
weeping and sweat comingle
 /on the march;
a hint of a tear slides
 /from heaven
raining a fixed witness written in ink
 /on walls.
Here history is written
with faces of hunger, of rage, of mourning,
written with arms, with soul, with ideals,
with solid letters, with a firm hand, with a slow stroke,
with the illusion that something better sets seed:
it is written in the heart of the martyrs.

Here death chooses masks with brave faces:
Isi Murillo, Pedro Magdiel, Róger Vallejo,
Pablo Hernández…

It is manifested among the people, embracing
 /softly,
while concealing its skeletal features.

La muerte mimetizada en escopeta,
en puño limpio, en culatazo,
transpirada en el humo de granadas y tanquetas
    /que acorralan.
Y zumban. Zumban las balas cruzando el cielo
    /antes limpito,
aniquilando toda estrella, toda luz, toda
    /posibilidad.
La canción de la muerte hace esfuerzos
    /por callarnos.
Y de nuevo vuelve la sed de sangre y de golpes.
La gente corre, grita y canta enardecida
un himno que ahora es doloroso, sentido,
lo cantan a pulmón vivo con el puño en alto
estrofa a estrofa, verso a verso, se invoca a los
héroes, se recuerda historia.
En los distintos puntos cardinales de nuestra
    /geografía
lo blanco se convierte en mugre, en color
    /de cobardía,
cobijando el odio de los que no aprendieron
    /a hacer otra cosa,
de los que disfrazan su deslealtad de amor
    /constitucional.

Y el pueblo en las calles resiste.
Agarrado del asfalto, de las piedras,
    /del que va a la par,
del que pasa, del que queda, del que cayó
    /en el camino
... de todo cuanto puedan agarrarse.
Porque sabe que tiene una posesión que nadie
habrá de quitarle nunca:
la certeza milenaria de que nadie más es dueño
    /de estas tierras.

Death blended into a shotgun,
a bare fist, a rifle butt,
sweating in the smoke of grenades and tanks
/that entrap.
And whiz. Bullets whiz, crisscrossing
/the once clear sky,
annihilating every star, all light, every
/possibility.
 The song of death tries
/to silence us.
And the thirst for blood and blows returns anew.
People run, scream and chant in a frenzy
a hymn that is now painful, sincere,
sung at the top of one's lungs and with raised fists
stanza by stanza, verse by verse, heroes evoked,
history remembered.
In the distinct cardinal points of our
/geography
white becomes filth, a color
/of cowardice,
sheltering the hate of those who did not learn
/a new way,
of those who disguise their lack of love for the
/constitution.

And the people in the streets resist.
Grasping the asphalt, the rocks,
/the person who marches alongside,
the one who continues, the one who stands, the one who fell
/along the way
.... everything they can hold onto.
Because the people know they possess something no one
can steal from them ever:
the millennial certainty that no one else is owner
/of these lands.

## I. En este país han secuestrado la verdad

En este país han secuestrado la verdad.
Debemos buscarla, con cautela,
en el bolsillo del saco nuevo del dictador,
debajo de las sillas del Congreso Nacional,
en las plantas de los zapatos de cada Diputado,
entre líneas en las cadenas nacionales,
en el atuendo sagrado del llamado Monseñor,
en las fosas de los cuarteles militares,
en lo más profundo de las conciencias
de cada uno de los golpistas,
en bodegas y sótanos de la tomada
      / Casa Presidencial,
en los juzgados: primero, segundo, tercero,
cuarto... los que sean necesarios,
en las oficinas de la Corte Suprema,
en la Fiscalía, en las casas de empresarios,
en las oficinas del Comisionado Nacional
de Derechos Humanos,
en medio de su polvosa colección
      /de balas de goma,
y, con mucho más detenimiento,
en los medios de (in) comunicación.
Será necesario exigir un Hábeas Corpus,
pegar afiches en medio de tantas manchas,
todo con tal de encontrarla.
No sea que en su afán de engañarnos,
la banda de secuestradores
termine pidiendo rescate.

## I. In This Country Truth Has Been Kidnapped

In this country truth has been kidnapped.
We should look for it, with caution,
in the pocket of the dictator's new jacket,
under the chairs in the National Congress,
on the soles of the shoes of every Legislator,
between the lines in the national media
in the sacred attire of the one called Monsignor,
in the graves at the military headquarters,
in the deepest part of the consciences
of each of the *golpistas*,
in the storerooms and basements of the seized
      /Presidential Palace,
in the courts: first, second, third,
fourth... as many as necessary,
in the offices of the Supreme Court,
in Justice, in the homes of entrepreneurs,
in the offices of the National Commission
for Human Rights,
in the middle of their dusty collection
      /of rubber bullets,
and, with even closer attention,
in the (mis)communication media.
It will be necessary to demand a Habeas Corpus,
glue posters in the middle of so many stains,
everything to try to find it.
Lest with their eagerness to deceive us,
the band of kidnappers
end up demanding a ransom.

## II. Nos recetaron el "aquí no pasa nada"

Nos recetaron el "aquí no pasa nada"
y lograron que sean muchos quienes lo crean.
Por eso, siguen visitando las tiendas y los cines,
para evadir la realidad que está allá lejos
      /en las pantallas
y en los lentes de gentes que fantasean
      /con una guerra lejana,
de reporteros que dicen lo que sus estómagos
      /les dictan.
Se falsea la verdad de tal manera que
      /hasta los diputados,
que se ocupan de asuntos tan elevados,
piensan que en las calles de nuestra ciudades
la gente corre tras mariposas de colores.
Por eso tiran piedras,
por eso miran al cielo,
por eso levantan el puño
y lloran de rabia porque no pueden alcanzarlas.

## II. They Prescribed to Us the "Nothing Is Happening Here"*

They prescribed to us the "nothing is happening here"
and they succeeded in getting many to believe it.
That is why they still visit the shops and cinemas,
to avoid reality that is remote
      /on the screens
and in the eyes of people who fantasize
      /with a war faraway,
and of reporters who say what their stomachs
      /tell them.
Truth is falsified in such a way that
      /even the legislators,
who take on such elevated matters,
think that in the streets of our cities
people chase after colorful butterflies.
That is why they throw rocks,
that is why they look at the sky,
that is why they raise their fist
and cry with rage because they cannot reach them.

*[Translations by Regina A. Root]*

---

\* Reference to official government statements during repression and resistance that there was no cause for alarm because, "Nothing is happening here."

# LETY ELVIR
## (San Pedro Sula, Cortés, 1966)

**Algunas íes sobre el golpe de estado**
*Estos muertos, estas muertas ya han huido de la muerte,*
*los asesinos jamás podrán huir de sus víctimas*
*aunque desconozcan del remordimiento y las culpas.*

Y de las cavernas salieron
con decretos y metrallas
con dictámenes y palos
con perros y cadenas
con cinismos y mentiras
con gases y tanquetas...
y vinieron hasta aquí.

# LETY ELVIR

Ph.D. candidate in Letters, National University of Costa Rica (Heredia, C.R.). Degrees in Letters from the National Autonomous University (UNAH) and Francisco Morazán National Pedagogical University (UPNFM). UNAH professor since 1996. Vice President of PEN-Honduras. Cofounder of the Casa Tomada literary workshop and of the National Association of Honduran Women Writers (ANDEH). Fulbright Scholar in Residence, Delaware State University, 2006-2007; founder and director of cultural page "Poesía Nómada" (Nomadic Poetry) in the bilingual newspaper, *El Tiempo Hispano*. Recipient of several literary prizes and recognitions. Featured author in the anthology, *Voces de mujeres en la literatura centroamericana* (Voices of Women in Central American Literature, University of Alcalá de Henares, Spain, 2012). Books published: *Luna que no cesa* (Moon That Ceases Not, 1998); *Mujer entre perro y lobo* (Woman Between Dog and Wolf/Between a Rock and a Hard Place, 2001); *Sublimes y perversos (cuentos)* (Sublime and Perverse (Stories), 2005); coauthor of *Mujeres en el mundo: Historia, revoluciones, dictaduras, trabajo, religión y poesía* (Women in the World: History, Revolutions, Dictatorships, Work, Religion and Poetry, University of Carabobo, Venezuela, 2007). Editor of the first edition of this anthology, *Honduras: Golpe y pluma. Antología de poesía resistente escrita por mujeres (2009-2013)* (Honduras: Coup and Pen. Anthology of Resistance Poetry Written by Women (2009-2013), 2013).

## Dotting Some I's Regarding the Coup
*These dead men, these dead women, have fled from death,*
*the assassins can never flee from their victims*
*though they disclaim remorse and blame.*

And from the caves they emerged
with decrees and machine guns
with pronouncements and clubs
with dogs and chains
with cynicisms and lies
with gases and tanks...
and came here.

Demonizaron libros, bibliotecas
transformaron el significado de las palabras
(sucesión constitucional, por Golpe de Estado
dictadura, por democracia
bala de goma, por balas que matan
cuatreros, chusma y mareros
por defensores de la patria,
son tan sólo unos ejemplos)
cambiaron el nombre
de las calles
y las vistieron de blanco
por fuera -mugre por dentro-
y las pintaron de rojo
cadáveres
mujeres violadas
costillas, hígados, pulmones
espaldas flageladas, manos y piernas fracturadas
dientes, brazos y zapatos quebrados.

Para entonces
ya se habían adueñado de gran parte del país
de las aceras, las plazas, puertos y universidades
de las urnas, las armas, los ríos y los mares
de los surcos del espacio, los *mass media* y del aire
de la leche de la infancia y los derechos de las mujeres
del Código del Trabajo y la Constitución de la República
de las tierras de indígenas, campesinado y garífunas
de las fichas de los jugadores y la sobriedad de los hombres
de los trapitos de la justicia y los legisladores
de los aeropuertos clandestinos y también los oficiales
(pero no pudieron robarse la alegría,
la esperanza
el ejemplo de Morazán y Lempira
Visitación Padilla y muchas más).

Y a pesar de tanta sangre derramada
sobre el pavimento, la maleza, los cañales
sobre la tierra polvorienta o en postas policiales
sobre el piso de alguna cárcel o casa de torturas
en el sótano del Congreso, en ambulancias u hospitales,

They demonized books, libraries
changed the meanings of words
(constitutional succession for Coup d'État,
dictatorship for democracy
rubber bullets for bullets that kill
traitors, mobs and gangs
for defenders of the homeland,
are just a few examples)
changed the names
of streets
and dressed them in white
on the outside –filth inside–
and painted them red
dead bodies
raped women
ribs, livers, lungs
backs whipped, hands and legs fractured
teeth, arms and shoes broken.

By then
they had already taken over most of the country
of the sidewalks, plazas, ports and universities
of the ballot boxes, firearms, rivers and seas
of the channels in space, the mass media and the air
of infants' milk and women's rights
of the Labor Code and the Constitution of the Republic
of the lands of the indigenous, farmers and Garífunas
of the game pieces of players and the sobriety of men
of the trappings of justice and legislators
of the clandestine airports and also the legal ones
(but they couldn't steal away the joy,
the hope
the example of Morazán and Lempira
of Visitación Padilla and many other women).

And despite so much blood spilled
over the pavement, the brush, the cane fields
over the dusty land or in police stations
over the floor of some jail or house of tortures
in the basement of the Congress, in ambulances or hospitals,

este pueblo se levanta, camina y marcha
sobre el siglo XXI
resiste, se enoja y canta
rescata a Honduras
y renueva el mundo.

*(21 de octubre, 2009)*

this people rises, walks and marches
into the 21st century
resists, grows angry and sings
rescues Honduras
and renews the world.

*(October 21, 2009)*

**Ustedes**

Ustedes, los que dejan hablar un rato
y luego mandan callar, masacrar, desaparecer
ustedes que entregaron Palmerola, la dignidad
ustedes, los que un día no tenían nada
ahora tienen todo lo que no les pertenece.
Ustedes, los que roban a los pobres
no tendrán paz para comer
para amar, ni para dormir.

Ustedes, usureros
invierten uno y sacan millones
ustedes, los mismos que robaron
los padres y las madres
a los niños, a las niñas de Honduras
y en emigrantes los convirtieron
ustedes, que como perros y buitres hambrientos
caen sobre las remesas de los exiliados del hambre
          y desempleo
de los que a la desesperación sometieron
y cruzaron océanos, desiertos, los trenes, las muertes
para trabajar como esclavos y sirvientes
ustedes que amasan fortunas
levantan sus castillos con la sangre de los pobres.

Ustedes, los que no creen
que la voz del pueblo es la de Dios
pero el pueblo lo sabe y dice:

*Mi palabra acusa tu maldad,*
*convoco a todas las familias*
*y vendrán una a una y construirán multitudes*
*destruirán la larva de la corrupción*
*corregirán al ladrón, al golpista*
*doblegarán la soberbia de los que se adueñaron de la voz*
*se alejaron del camino de la decencia*
*violaron las leyes, se llenaron de condecoraciones*
*y azotaron a las hijas y a los hijos del pueblo.*

Ay de aquellos que no creen que las montañas

**You People**

You people, who let others talk for a while
and then order them silenced, massacred, disappeared
you, who surrendered Palmerola, dignity
you, who once had nothing
now have everything that doesn't belong to you.
You, who rob the poor
will have no peace to eat
to love, not even to sleep.

You, usurers
invest one and get back millions
you, the same ones who stole
fathers and mothers
from the boys, from the girls of Honduras
and turned them into emigrants
you, who like hungry dogs and vultures
pounce on the remittances from those exiled by hunger
       and unemployment
from those you pushed into desperation
and who crossed oceans, deserts, trains, deaths
to work as slaves and servants
you, who amass fortunes
build your castles with the blood of the poor.

You, who don't believe
that the voice of the people is that of God
but the people know and say:

*My word denounces your evil,*
*I call together all the families*
*that will join, one by one, and become multitudes*
*will destroy the larva of corruption*
*castigate the thief, the golpista*
*crush the arrogance of those who seized the voice*
*strayed from the path of decency*
*broke laws, covered themselves with medals*
*and whipped the daughters and sons of the people.*

Beware, those who don't believe that mountains

encierran lava, fuego y otros misterios.
Ay de ustedes,
los que construyen caminos de dolor y aflicción
encarcelan, exilian, torturan, asesinan escritores
periodistas, profesores, aborígenes, defensores
homosexuales, mujeres, pobladores, artistas
y amontonan el oro y la plata.
Ay de ustedes, que todo lo borran o incendian
todo lo tapan como el gato a su pestilencia
que piden el voto y luego traicionan a quienes se los dan
ustedes, que se reparten la patria cual si fuera
un pastel de fresa y chocolate
ustedes, que fruncen el ceño y llaman la policía
cuando la juventud se amotina
las mujeres se rebelan
o cuando los campesinos e indígenas reclaman la tierra
o los fiscales en huelga de hambre, la decencia
ustedes que comulgan y se liberan de pecados
los domingos después del futbol
a cambio de la bula o la burla de los dioses
ay de ustedes, los que se reúnen en la sombra
a preparar la siguiente mordida
al famélico y al desnutrido.

Ustedes no tienen nombre ni partido
- pero sabemos sus apellidos-
ustedes no tienen raza ni religión
pero adoran el dinero, su único dios.

Ay de ustedes que nos roban el reino de la tierra
y nos piden que esperemos cabizbajos
por donde salen la Luna y el Sol
ay de ustedes, los que han olvidado
que abundan las agujas y sus ojos les esperan
ay de ustedes, los que ven la copa de un sombrero
donde en realidad hay un volcán
ay de ustedes, los que olvidan
que aquí hay hambre de justicia y pan,
que todo lo que inicia tiene su final.

*(2009, 2011, 2013)*

hide lava, fire and other mysteries.
Beware, you people
who build paths of pain and affliction
who imprison, exile, torture, murder writers
journalists, professors, natives, defenders
homosexuals, women, settlers, artists
and pile up gold and silver.
Beware, you people who erase or burn everything
cover up everything like a cat his own stench
who ask for votes and then betray those who give them
you, who divide up the country as if it were
a cake of strawberry and chocolate
you, who frown and call the police
when youths riot
or women rebel
or when farmers and indigenous people demand the land
or public prosecutors on a hunger strike, decency
you, who take communion and free yourselves of sin
on Sundays after soccer matches
through dispensation or derision of the gods
beware, you who meet in darkness
to plot the next bite
out of the famished and the malnourished.

You have no name or party
–but we know your names–
you have no race or religion
but you worship money, your only god.

Beware, you who steal from us the kingdom on earth
and ask us to wait, heads bowed,
where the Moon and the Sun rise
beware, you who have forgotten
that needles abound and your eyes await them
beware, you who see the crown of a hat
where there is actually a volcano
beware, you who forget
that here there is hunger for justice and bread,
that everything begun comes to its end.

    *(2009, 2011, 2013)*

## Los muertos en mi país

De un tiempo para acá
los muertos en mi país
están por todos lados
en los basureros, en las cunetas
en los hospitales, en los presidios,
en el aire, en los sueños
en las montañas, en los arrabales,
flotan en los ríos, en los mares
como peces envenenados
o ballenas suicidas.

Son como piedras
se tropieza con ellos
estorban el paso
interrumpen el tráfico
estropean los planes, horarios.
Están en el café, el agua, la comida
en los periódicos de lunes a sábado y los dominicales
se conversa con ellos, se habla de ellas
de velorio en velorio
de entierro en entierro
de lágrima en lágrima
caen por docenas como moscas en cachaza
sin contar con los que no aparecen
ni en morgues o reportes policiales.

Los muertos en mi país
a veces no salen, se cansan,
juegan a las escondidas
en bolsas de plástico, cajas de cartón
o están en trocitos regados por ahí

Y se les llora tanto y se les extraña tanto.

## The Dead in My Country

For some time now
the dead in my country
are everywhere
in dumps, in ditches
in hospitals, in prisons,
in the air, in dreams
in the mountains, in the slums,
floating in rivers, in seas
like poisoned fish
or suicidal whales.

They are like rocks
you trip over them
they block your path
stop traffic
mess up plans, schedules.
They are in coffee, water, food
in the newspapers from Monday to Saturday and the
                                        Sunday editions
we talk with them, talk about the women
from funeral wake to funeral wake
from burial to burial
from tear to tear
they drop by the dozen like flies into syrup
not counting the ones that don't appear
in morgues or police reports.

The dead in my country
occasionally don't leave, they get tired,
play hide-and-seek
in plastic bags, cardboard boxes
or appear in pieces strewn about.

And they are cried over and missed so terribly.

Los muertos en mi país
no mueren de viejos
sino de impunidad y violencia
de balas de plomo y más plomo
bum bum bum de día y de noche
casquillos regados igual que los muertos.
Retuerzo las manos, el mapa, cintas amarillas
chorrea la sangre, llueve sangre en mi país

Los muertos son tantos
no cabe su ausencia, no cabe su olor
los muertos son tantos
no cabe el miedo, no cabe el dolor.

*(2012, febrero 2013)*

The dead in my country
don't die from old age
but from impunity and violence
bullets of lead and more lead
boom boom boom day and night
shell casings strewn like the dead.
I wring my hands, the map, yellow ribbons,
blood spews, blood rains in my country

The dead are so many
their absence is too much, their smell is too much
the dead are so many
the fear is too much, the pain is too much.

*(2012, February 2013)*


*[Translations by María Roof]*

## REYNA ESCOBAR TRIGUEROS
(Tela, Atlántida, 1960)


(NO PHOTOGRAPH AT POET´S REQUEST)


**HUESOS DE METAL**

Luces apagadas, ojos cerrados, sueños cortados
dolor de hambre, ansiedad por la mañana
más que vivir, sobrevivir.

Y en toda esta mezcla
*hay un monstruo con huesos de metal*
que suena todo el día y se convierte en una pesadilla

Yo no sé si es el llanto de los hijos,
el grito del marido,
o el ruido de estas máquinas
pero no escucho....
Sólo puedo pensar cómo terminar esta meta
temprano

¿Cómo escuchar el canto de las aves?
¿Cómo escuchar mi música interna?
¿Cuándo tendré un poco de descanso?

¿Cuándo dejaré de sobrevivir
para vivir, vivir, vivir?

## REYNA ESCOBAR TRIGUEROS

Legal advocate for 10 years with the Honduran Women's Collective (CODEMUH). A former worker in the maquila assembly industry in the northern part of the country, she has dedicated herself to the defense of women's rights, particularly of maquila workers. She writes poems that show her social class consciousness, her experience and direct condemnation of the extreme exploitation women suffer in the maquilas, where owners fail to comply with the most elemental norms established by the Labor Code, a situation that has deteriorated since the 2009 coup d'etat.

## BONES OF STEEL

Lights extinguished, eyes closed, dreams cut short
hunger pangs, eagerness for morning
more than to live, to survive.

And in all this mix
*there is a monster with bones of steel*
that rumbles all day and becomes a nightmare

I don't know if it's the cries of my children,
the shout of my husband,
or the noise of these machines
but I don't hear....
I can only think about how to finish my quota
early.

How can I hear the song of birds?
How can I hear my inner music?
When will I get a little rest?

When will I stop surviving
in order to live, live, live?

*[Translation by Regina A. Root]*

## DIANA ESPINAL MEZA
### (Tegucigalpa, 1964)

**Lázaro se levanta**

Hoy hizo erupción
un búfalo de fauces cuadradas

Hoy pide ser amamantado el siglo XXI

Enjambres de botas y un estado inaceptable de trombas
ofrendan trombas al viento

Hoy hizo erupción un búfalo de fauces cobrizas
en la cara llevaba un antifaz de cáncer
que ahuyentaba los reflejos, las oportunidades,
la estación de los espejos

Hoy pide ser amamantado el siglo XXI
se levantó Lázaro con su ropaje de hormigas
alguien saca sus viejas cuentas de vidrio molido
alguien coagula chillidos de bisagra

En la despensa del miedo
hay hemorragias que violan sueños.

**DIANA ESPINAL MEZA**

Poet residing in Ciudad Juárez, Chihuahua, México, and pursuing graduate studies. Degree in Literature, Francisco Morazán National Pedagogical University (UPNFM); certificate in Poetry, escritores.org, Barcelona, Spain; diploma in History, Autonomous University of Ciudad Juárez, México. International representative of the National Association of Honduran Women Writers (ANDEH) and of the Peruvian Casa del Poeta. Four books of poetry: *Del ladrido del sombrero a la escama del sol* (From the Bark of the Hat to the Scale of the Sun, 2007); *Tras los hilos* (After the Threads, 2004); *Eclipse de agujas* (Eclipse of Needles, 2000); *Reiteración de cornisas* (Reiteration of Cornises, forthcoming).

**Lazarus Rises**

Today there erupted
a buffalo of square jaws

Today the twenty-first century asks to be suckled

Swarms of boots and an unacceptable state of cloudbursts
offer downpours to the wind

Today the buffalo of coppery jaws erupted
its face covered with a cancerous mask
that scared away reflections, opportunities,
the season of mirrors

Today the twenty-first century asks to be suckled
Lazarus rose with his robes of ants
someone takes out his old beads of ground glass
someone coagulates the cry of hinges

In the dispensing of fear
are hemorrhages that violate dreams.

**Se ha quedado varado**

Se ha quedado varado
Aquel punto vulnerable de acuarelas

Como el silencio al hambre
Hay dígitos que faltos de estallidos
Pero embusteros de patios
Se entrelazan en brillos verticales para sacar néctar
        a destiempo

Se ha quedado varado
El perfil idiota del malvado
Y
La sangre cual si fuera arena grazna

Como el óxido al olvido
Perdimos memoria y ganamos mortaja
Perdimos luz y ganamos estiércol
Perdimos balance y ganamos espanto

Hay guadañas que prometen roces
Y
Hay roces que matan

**It's Ended Up Stranded**

It's ended up stranded
That vulnerable point of watercolors

Like silence to hunger
There are digits which lacking explosions
Yet patio liars
Interweave in vertical brilliance to extract nectar
         at the wrong time

It's ended up stranded
The idiotic profile of the evil one
And
Blood caws as if it were sand

Like rust to oblivion
We lost memory and we gained a shroud
We lost light and we gained manure
We lost balance and we gained fear

There are scythes that promise touches
And
There are touches that kill

## Este monosílabo de piedra

Este monosílabo de piedra
No dobla bisagras y la estación de avispas se siente
        como ballesta de agua
En estos días todo pasa y pasa en espirales de hormigas
Cadenas de marimbas
Tardes que se despeñan
Altas mareas en el asfalto
Horizonte acuchillado
Filo de hacha protuberancia y eje

Esta corona de fuego tiene la espalda negra
Se niega a consumirse
Abre las piernas y aborta escarcha

Tegucigalpa es aleteo de voces
De letras de manos
Tegucigalpa es tiempo sostenido en plomizos buzones
        y en acuarios de vidrio.

## This Monosyllable of Stone

This monosyllable of stone
Doesn't bend hinges and the season of wasps is felt
      like a water cannon
These days all things happen and pass in spirals of ants
Chains of marimbas
Evenings that crumble
High tides on the asphalt
The horizon stabbed
The axe blade a bulge and axis

This crown of fire shows its black spine
Refuses to consume itself
Opens its legs and aborts frost

Tegucigalpa is fluttering with voices
And letters from hands
Tegucigalpa is time sustained in metal letter boxes
      and glass aquariums.


*[Translations by Regina A. Root]*

**INDIRA FLAMENCO**
(La Ceiba, Atlántida, 1969)

**Reencuentro**
*Para los militares golpistas*

Aquel General
de pies
condenados por la historia,
pide perdón desde el exilio.
Pero las madres de la plaza de Mayo
escupen su rostro
hasta cubrirlo con el mar de los espejos.
En esta acción conciliatoria
se desparraman sus vísceras.

## INDIRA FLAMENCO

Poet, cultural promoter and educator, Degree in Letters, National Autonomous University (UNAH). Author of ethnographic studies of the Garífunas in the northern part of the country. Author of the book of poems *Cuando las rocas fecundan el llanto* (When Rocks Fertilize Weeping, 2002). Resident of San Pedro Sula since childhood.

### Reencounter
*To the military* golpistas

That General
with feet
condemned by history,
begs forgiveness from exile.
But mothers of the Plaza de Mayo
spit in his face
until it's covered with the sea of mirrors.
In this conciliatory action
his guts are spilled.

**El altar frente al espejo**

Si vivieras, mi señor Kinich,
si transitaras por las calles
de esta patria tuya, nuestra,
un llanto hueco moriría en tu garganta.
Si volvieras,
fundador Kuk Mo,
en el hálito de un chamán verdadero,
tus ojos de infinito llorarían.

Decapitarías, yo lo sé,
a los golpistas civiles y militares,
que se sientan como reyes del Hol Pop,
para acuchillar lentamente a nuestro pueblo.

## Altar Facing the Mirror

If you lived, my sir Kinich,
if you walked along the streets
of this, your, our, fatherland
a hollow cry would die in your throat.
If you came back,
founder Kuk Mo,
in the breath of a true shaman,
your infinite eyes would cry.

You would behead, I know,
the civilian and military *golpistas*,
that sit like kings of the Hol Pop,
to slowly stab our people to death.

## Salutación a los golpistas

Agazapados en complicidad con la inmundicia
se retuercen los golpistas,
con palabras desteñidas y la justicia ultrajada
abren sus fauces del dinosaurio hambriento
para desfigurar el pueblo a dentelladas.
Construyen cercos de represión
y contemplan desde su juego mediático
el grito ensordecedor de los humildes...
Encierran el sol en sus casas blindadas
cercenan la verdad y la visten con su andamiaje
de calumnias
con el espejismo de engañarnos.
Sin embargo,
a pesar de la lluvia matutina, de las golpizas
callejeras
y la avanzada de terror de los secuaces,
el pueblo no sucumbe,
en marchas titánicas hilvanan la esperanza
denuncian con ahínco la injusticia
levantan antorchas de dignidad perdida
y lanzan dardos en llamas
a los enemigos de la patria.

## Salutation to the *Golpistas*

Crouched, in collusion with filth
the *golpistas* writhe,
with faded words and defiled justice,
they open their jaws like the hungry dinosaur
to disfigure the people with their teeth.
They build fences of repression
and gaze from their media game upon
the deafening cry of the humble...
They lock the sun in their armored houses
mutilate the truth and dress it with their scaffolding
of calumnies
with the illusion of deceiving us.
However,
despite the morning rain, beatings
in the streets
and the terror attack by henchmen,
the people do not succumb,
in titanic parades they weave hope
vigorously denounce injustice,
raise torches of lost dignity
and throw flaming darts
at the enemies of the fatherland.


*[Translation by Andrea Gaytán Cuesta]*

## DAYSI FLORES
### (Tegucigalpa, 1978)

**Impotente**

El sonido del viento sabe a magenta
La luz murmura suavemente su canto

Brujas del sur me observan impetuosas
Intento escapar de esta realidad
Con sabor a Golpe, represión, gas y muerte

Los cascabeles olorosos a tormenta, se burlan
La lluvia suena a ternura
Me rindo
Y una vez más...

¡¡GRITO!!

## DAYSI FLORES

Civil Engineering degree, Latina University of Costa Rica. Member of Just Associates (JASS), an international feminist movement building organization, and of the National Network of Women Human Rights Defenders. Social media and communication expert.

### Impotent

The sound of the wind tastes like magenta
Light gently whispers its song

Witches of the south observe me intensely
I try to escape this reality
That tastes of Coup, repression, gas, and death

Rattles smelling of storms make fun
The rain sounds like tenderness
I surrender
And once again...

I SCREAM!!

**Imprudente**

Tu inhóspita existencia me marca
mis vísceras se llenan de un líquido verde...
amargo como tus uniformes

En un instante todo cambia
busco más sonrisas, más voces
más gritos de libertad

Salgo de nuevo a las calles
pongo mi rabia junto a mis colores
grito hasta quedarme sin voz

Lucho como todas
como antes...
como NUNCA!!

**Imprudent**

Your inhospitable existence marks me
my entrails fill with green liquid...
bitter like your uniforms

In an instant everything changes
I seek more smiles, more voices
more cries for freedom

I go again into the streets
I unite my anger with my colors
I scream until I lose my voice

I fight like all women
like before...
like NEVER BEFORE!

**Leo**

Hoy
tu recuerdo asaltó mi existencia al compás de un café
llegaste huyendo de un Golpe Militar

Con el sabor amargo de la locura y el dolor
compartiste historias lejanas y distantes
llenas de acordes de guitarra empapados de luchas diarias
        y amor

Como burla inimaginada del destino
que deja en mi alma, vacíos inexplicables
la crueldad de mi propio Golpe te llevó
grito en las calles llena de rabia por tu ausencia
con la misma voz desafinada que gritaba en tu ventana
y, a veces, siento que mis alas vuelan hasta tocar tu existencia

Sé que no estás... que no volverás.
Aun así, en cada calle
en cada café
te sigo sintiendo
te sigo viendo.
Una parte de mi... Te sigue esperando.

**Leo**[*]

Today
your memory attacked my existence to the rhythm of a coffee
you arrived fleeing from a Military Coup

With the bitter flavor of madness and pain
you shared remote, distant stories
full of guitar chords drenched with daily struggles
      and love

As an unimagined mockery of fate
that leaves in my soul unexplainable voids
the cruelty of my own Coup took you away
I scream in the streets filled with rage because of your absence
with the same out of tune voice that screamed in your window
and, sometimes, I feel my wings fly until they touch your existence

I know that you are not here... that you will not return.
Even so, in every street
in every café
I keep feeling you
I keep seeing you.
A part of me... Keeps waiting for you

*[Translations by Andrew Bentley]*

---

[*] Leo: Leonardo Gilmet Kennedy, immigrated to Honduras for political reasons during the dictatorship in his native Uruguay. Deeply affected by the June 2009 coup d´état, he took his own life three months later, in September.

## ARMIDA GARCÍA AGUILAR
### (Tegucigalpa, 1971)

**II**

Este caldo
de tuercas con zapatos,
de brazos con amortiguadores;
de hombres que lanzan fuego
por los ojos
y cuervos con las alas
soldadas a la tierra.
Para creer en algo,
en este cielo con goteras,
hay que coser las hojas
a los hombros de las ceibas.

# ARMIDA GARCÍA AGUILAR

Degree in Letters, National Autonomous University (UNAH). Co-organizer of the Dissident's Turn International Poetry Festival (El turno del disidente). Awarded the 1994 Golden Lyre Poetry Prize by the Ideas Group. Former member of the rock group "Eve's Triangle" (El Triángulo de Eva). Author of *La soledad justificada* (Justified Solitude, 1997). These poems are from the unpublished book *Tragadores de fuego* (Fire Swallowers).

## II

This broth
of shoe-clad wingnuts
of shock absorber arms
of men whose eyes
shoot flames
and crows with wings
welded to the ground.
In order to believe in anything,
in this dripping sky,
you have to sew leaves
onto the shoulders of silk-cotton trees.

## XX

Tierra sin puntos cardinales
de casas con muletas
que se baten en los acantilados,
de cactus que florecen
en la boca de los perros
y amantes que dan en adopción
los platos.

Aquí
el cielo es angosto,
tanto,
que los cuervos tapan el sol
con los dedos.

## XX

Land without cardinal points,
of houses on crutches
that pound against cliffs,
of cacti that bloom
in the mouths of dogs
and lovers that give up dishes
for adoption.

Here
the sky is narrow,
so narrow,
that crows cover up the sun
with their fingers.

## XXI

Aquí
el día es un andamio sin orillas
donde los gatos conspiran,
irascibles,
contra las antenas.
Las azoteas vigilan,
sin credencial,
nadie se atreve a soñar
con el canto maternal de las ballenas.

## XXI

Here
a day is a scaffolding without edges
where cats hatch plots,
grumpily,
against antennas.
The terraces keep watch,
without authorization,
no one dares to dream
of the maternal songs of whales.


*[Translations by Jonathan Arries]*

# BLANCA GUIFARRO
## (Catacamas, Olancho, 1946)

**Caza Blanca en tres actos**

I acto
He visto recorrer
la tristeza
en cada cuerpo sin cuerpo
esqueletos
que piden agua
y reclaman sin hablar
padecen de dolor
sin haberlo deseado

II acto
no logras detener
tu afán expansivo
allí
donde pones las garras
rompes la vida
allí donde compras conciencias
destruyes los pueblos

**BLANCA GUIFARRO**

Sociologist and retired professor, National Autonomous University (UNAH); creator and professor of the UNAH Women´s Studies curriculum. Founder and director of the journal *Entre Amigas* (Between Friends), 1992-1997. Author and editor of *Hojas al viento* (Leaves in the Wind), that published 20 issues, 1998-2007. Poetry books published: *La otra... mitad* (The Other...Half, 1996); *Ataduras sueltas* (Loose Ties, 1998); *Los versos están en todas partes* (Verses Are Everywhere, 2004); *Apegos en mi mayor* (Attachments in E Major, 2007); *Metáforas de fuego* (Metaphors of Fire, 2009); *Versos en resistencia* (Verses in Resistance, 2009); *Con mis manos* (With My Hands, 2010); *Para no olvidar* (So As Not to Forget, 2011) and *Espío por tu cuerpo, recorro sus veredas* (I Watch for Your Body, Walk Along Its Trails, 2013).

**White House Hunt in Three Acts**[*]

act I
I have seen
sadness penetrate
in each body without a body
skeletons
that ask for water
and protest without speaking
they suffer in pain
without having wanted this

act II
you cannot control
your endless ambition
wherever
your talons strike
you shatter life
wherever you purchase consciences
you destroy communities

---

[*] The title plays on the poet's first name and on the common term, "Casa Blanca," White House, and the unusual, "Caza Blanca," literally, White Hunt.

III acto
eres camaleón experimentado
te metes
donde no te llaman
y aunque te sollen el rabo
sigues
dándole cuerda
a tu "divina comedia"

act III
an experienced chameleon
you go
where you aren't invited
and even when someone shreds your tail
you keep your
"divine comedy"
playing on and on.

**Valle del Aguán**

Me duele el dolor
del valle florido
herido de muerte
en el juego perverso
de las acumulaciones
dolor
que se agiganta
en cada noche
durmiendo insomne
en cada mañana
con la mesa sin patas
en cada año
cerrando y abriendo
torbellinos
me duele el dolor
provocado
por colmillos de patriarcas
metidos
en el ombligo fértil
de la tierra
atrapada en la garganta
sin fondo
proyectada
en dólares, chantaje
compra y desapariciones
a su vez
cuerpos escuálidos
batidos en el lodo
que dejan su piel
en alambres de púa
renacen conciencias
no se venden
no se compran
crecen
cual
gigantescas palmeras
capaces de paralizar
y hacer palidecer

## Aguan River Valley

I suffer the pain
of the flowering valley
mortally wounded
in the perverse game
of accumulation
pain
that grows
every night
sleeping awake
every morning
at the legless table
every year
ending and beginning
whirlwinds
I suffer the pain
caused
by the fangs of patriarchs
sunken
into the fertile womb
of the earth
caught in the gullet
that is bottomless
calculated
in dollars, blackmail
sales and disappearances
one after the other
emaciated bodies
beaten muddied
that leave their flesh
on barbed wire
consciences are reborn
neither for sale
nor purchase
they grow
like
giant palm trees
able to paralyze
and strike fear in

al sátrapa
come Matria-Patria
en la succión
de sangre colectiva
me duele el dolor
que encarna
mío, mío, mío
sadismo que resbala
en carcajadas
al provocar palizas y torturas
hombres abrigados
con odio
listos para derramar
la bilis del patrón
me duele el dolor
de nuevas vidas
generaciones
que la maleza quema
y el sabor a educación, tierra y ternura
postergada...
me duele el dolor del valle
fértil de ilusiones
movido en el juego
YO soy el poder
en contrapartida
NOSOTROS
Y NOSOTRAS
desnudamos
su poder

the tyrant
Mother/Fatherland devourer
sucking
the collective blood
I suffer the pain
he embodies
mine, mine, mine
sadism that breaks
into laughter
ordering beatings and tortures
men cloaked
in hatred
prepared to spill
the boss's bile
I suffer the pain
of new lives
generations
that the evil weed burns
and the taste of education, land and compassion
deferred...
I suffer the pain of the valley
fertile in illusions
put into play in the game
"I am power"
however
WE MEN
AND WE WOMEN
strip him of
his power

**Wendy**

Recorriste calles
avenidas, bulevares
colonias y barrios
haciendo sentir tu conciencia
confundida en la multitud
sólo las bombas genocidas
detuvieron tu vuelo
estás en los senderos
del tiempo
tu nueva morada
tendrá sabor a tus pasos
podrás
hacerle trenzas a la luna
y acariciar su cintura
alimentarte con sopa de olla
mondongo y tapado
perfumes de libertad
jugarás cucumbé
con las constelaciones
y tu nombre quedará grabado
en la eternidad del firmamento
a tu corta edad
compartiste
con gladiolas, crisantemos
y margaritas
te fuiste
y la lucha continúa
sin encontrar aún
el cordón umbilical
cercenado el 28 de Junio

**Wendy**

You ran down streets
avenues, boulevards
neighborhoods and barrios
making known your conscience
lost in the crowd
only the genocidal bombs
stopped your flight
you are on the paths
of time
your new dwelling
will be perfumed at your step
you can
make braids for the moon
and caress her waist
feast on Sunday stew
of tripe and pork
aromas of freedom
you will play hide-and-seek
with the constellations
and your name will be forever written
across heaven's eternity
at your young age
you shared
with gladiolas, chrysanthemums
and daisies
you left
and the struggle continues
without finding yet
the umbilical cord
severed on the 28th of June


*[Translations by Jonathan Arries]*

# DORIS AMANDA HENRÍQUEZ
(Gracias, Lempira, 1991)

**A mí no me lo contaron**

Recuerdo muy bien
esos días de *toque de queda*
sentía un repudio dentro de mi alma.
Vi rostros rebosantes de angustia
gente enardecida
también mortales vacíos.

Duele recordar
no es que me guste el dolor
pero estoy con la osadía de no olvidar
para sentirme viva.

Veo en cada plantón
el renacer de una nueva era.
He dejado la camisa de fuerza
he dejado el silencio
he dejado el olvido.

Cada día la decisión de rebelarme
ante los abusos es más patente.
Andaré por las calles
las mismas que muchos obreros han caminado
donde las luchas han tomado fuerza
señalando a los opresores.

Me queda la esperanza
la certeza que no estoy sola
que cada día habrá una lucha
y que más de una sombra
caminará junto a mí.

# DORIS AMANDA HENRÍQUEZ

Elementary school teacher; Education student, National Autonomous University (UNAH). Member of the ARTE-UNAH national folkloric dance group, with performances in national and international venues. Participant in the II International Northeast Regional Dance Festival 2012 that was held in several Mexican states.

## They Didn't Tell Me

I remember very well
those days of curfew
I felt disgust within my soul.
I saw faces overflowing with anguish
infuriated people
as well as empty mortals.

Remembering hurts
it's not that I like pain
but audaciously I chose not to forget
so that I feel alive

I picture in each seedling
the rebirth of a new era
I have set aside the straitjacket
I have set aside silence
I have set aside oblivion.

Every day the decision to rebel
against abuses is clearer.
I will walk the streets
the same ones where so many workers have marched
and struggles have gained strength
by pointing at the oppressors.

My hope remains
the certainty that I am not alone
that every day there will be a battle
and that more than one shadow
will walk alongside me.

*[Translation by Marie Pfaff]*

## SOFÍA ALEJANDRA HERNÁNDEZ MOTIÑO
### (Gracias, Lempira, 1991)

**En mis entrañas te llevo golpe**

En mis entrañas te llevo golpe
la pavorosa fecha de tu arribo es mi sombra
aun me dueles, aun te lloro
hoy mi memoria roció el recuerdo de la gris mañana
que abolió la esperanza de mi pueblo
dos hijas gemelas de un estado de derecho libre mueren
mis amadas amigas Temis y Democracia
son veladas en la boca de un congreso
mi nación está en llanto y despojada de sueños
bramar la injusticia es el único remedio
frente al cielo testigo del putrefacto hecho
donde en un campo de batalla
nobles pierden su vida
muere con ellos su gran amor a mi patria.
Cae lluvia de sangre en las calles de mi Honduras
corrientes de esperanza, ilusiones e ideas
terminan en cunetas
mi pueblo tan solo queda en sed de Justicia y Paz
pues una mujer corrupta con velo blanco acobija mi pueblo
pero una lucha nace
un nuevo horizonte se asoma
en las faldas de mi pueblo
mujeres y hombres dignos y valientes
perfumados en sudor
corren a los caminos de luchar
armados de principios y convicciones
en las calles nubadas de gases
tan solo por el anhelo de ver
a mi Honduras Libre...

# SOFÍA ALEJANDRA HERNÁNDEZ MOTIÑO

Law Student at the National Autonomous University of Honduras (UNAH). Member of the literary group, "Women of Today" ("Las de hoy").

## I Carry You Inside Me, Coup

I carry you inside me, coup
the dreadful date of your arrival is my shadow
you still hurt me, I still cry
today my mind touched the memory of the grey morning
that crushed the hope of my people
two twin daughters of a free state of law perish
my beloved friends Themis and Democracy
are mourned only in word by a congress
my nation is in tears and stripped of dreams
decrying injustice is the only recourse
beneath the sky that witnessed the putrid act
where on a battlefield
nobles lose their lives
dying with them their great love for my country.
Rain of blood falls on the streets of my Honduras
torrents of hope, illusions, and ideas
run into ditches
my lonely people can only thirst for Justice and Peace
for a corrupt woman with a white veil covers my people
but a struggle is born
a new horizon appears
in the hillsides of my people
women and men worthy and brave
perfumed in sweat
take to the street to fight
armed with principles and convictions
in the roads clouded with gases
longing only to see
my Honduras Free...

[Translation by Andrew Bentley]

# KARLA LARA
(Tegucigalpa, 1968)

## A Manuel
*(Manuel Flores, profesor asesinado frente a sus alumnas y alumnos en el Instituto en el que trabajaba, miembro del Partido Socialista Centroamericano)*

Caminabas calles,
regabas ideas, Manuel
el pañuelo al cuello,
el morral al hombro, Manuel

Letra insurrecta,
palabra certera, Manuel
y era tu sonrisa
como agua fresca, Manuel

Hoy gritó María
hoy marchó la Juana
hoy se alzaron tantas, Manuel
y esa es tu forma de seguir luchando, Manuel

# KARLA LARA

Singer-songwriter, feminist, militant. Born and raised among artists, songs and poems. Former member of the Choir at the National Autonomous University (UNAH); performer with "Rascaniguas," "Doble Vía," and "Trovasón." Singer for eight years with the Salvadoran groups, "Cutumay Camones" and "Los del Oficio." Solo performer since 2002, recording the albums *Dónde andar* (Where to Walk, 2004), *Antes del puente* (Before the Bridge, 2008), and *Recordarles* (Remember Them, 2013). Producer for the radio program "Sin café no hay mañana" (Without Coffee, There's No Morning) for the Coffee Growers Cooperatives of Honduras. Participant in the 2008 prosecutors' hunger strike at the National Congress, demanding the trial and sentencing of corrupt officials. She has performed internationally throughout Central America, Argentina, Ecuador, the United States, Canada, Denmark, Spain, Trinidad and Tobago, and in other venues.


**To Manuel**
*(Manuel Flores, a teacher who was murdered in front of his students at the high school where he worked. He was a member of the Socialist Party of Central America)*

You took it to the streets
and sowed ideas, Manuel
bandana around your neck,
bag over your shoulder, Manuel

Letters of rebellion
your word so true, Manuel
and your smile, a smile
like cool, sweet water, Manuel

María joined in the chants today
and Juana in the march, Manuel
so many girls joined in today,
your struggle is theirs, Manuel

Hoy gritó María
hoy marchó la Juana
hoy se alzaron tantos, Manuel
y esa es tu forma de seguir con vida

Tu figura grande
y corazón izquierdo, Manuel
parecías hippie
o como un buen Cristo, Manuel

En las calles gritan
tu nombre es consigna, Manuel
y en la escuela, el barrio
se te extraña tanto, Manuel.

*(2010)*

María joined in the chants today
and Juana in the march
so many boys joined in today,
you live on in them, Manuel

You were so tall,
and your leftist heart so large, Manuel
you were like some hippy
or like sweet Jesus himself, Manuel

They chant in the streets
it´s your name they chant, Manuel
and in our school and in our barrio
we miss you so much, Manuel.

    (2010)

**Recordarles**
> *(En el marco del XXX Aniversario del COFADEH)*

Recordarles, nombrarles
para nunca olvidarles
y que en nuestra memoria
siempre ocupen un lugar

Salvar en los recuerdos
sus ejemplos,
sanar en nuestras almas
el dolor de sus ausencias

Traerles, nombrarles
para siempre recordarles
y que en todas las luchas
siempre tengan su sitial

Salvar en los ejemplos
sus recuerdos
sanar en nuestras almas
esta ausencia de justicia

Tu nombre, consigna en las calles
tus manos, la caricia que no tengo

Tu imagen, viva flor de la esperanza
tu risa, la luz que me hace falta

Tus sueños, alas que izan nuestro vuelo
tu vida, la bondad arrebatada

Tu nombre, grito limpio que se alza
tu boca, es el beso que me dabas

## Remember Them
### *(On the 30th anniversary of COFADEH*)*

Let's remember them, call their names
so we never forget them
and so they will always
have a place in our memory

May their examples
remain in our memory
and may we find healing in our souls
for the pain of our loss

Let's recall their names, say them
so we remember them forever
and so in our every struggle
they will take their place

May their memory
remain as examples
and may we find healing in our souls
for this lack of justice

Your name, chanted in the streets
your hands, the caress that I miss

Your image, live flower of hope
your laughter, the light I so need

Your dreams, wings to lift our flight
your life, goodness snatched away

Your name, a chant loud and clear
your lips, the kisses you gave me

---

* Committee of Relatives of Disappeared Detainees in Honduras, founded in 1982.

Honrarles, cantarles
para siempre acompañarles
y que en nuestra historia
la verdad no calle más

Sanar el corazón
si se quebranta
salvar en nuestras vidas
el amor y la confianza

Let's honor them, sing to them,
so we are with them always
and in our history
may truth be silenced no more.

May the heart be healed
if broken
may love and hope
endure in our lives

**Cajas de recuerdos...**
> *(para Marcela, Mauro y Sergio, mi hija y mis hijos que tuvieron que irse de Honduras)*

Guardé en cajas los recuerdos
que a tu regreso abrirás
para que vuelvan los momentos
que el tiempo nos quiera borrar

Alguna foto, una tarjeta
que le hiciste a tu mamá
algún poema a medio palo
esta canción sin terminar

Una gorra, un banderín
un panfleto, un boletín
alguna de esas armas peligrosas
que te arrancaron de mi...

Y dónde pongo tu sonrisa
si ya no hay cajas pa'l dolor
y dónde guardo la nostalgia
si yo respiro, es tu olor

La locura de soñar
la contracultura de pensar
alguna de esas alas amorosas
que nos van a reencontrar

Guardé en cajas los recuerdos....

## Memory Boxes...
> *(For Marcela, Mauro, Sergio, my daughter and my sons who had to flee Honduras)*

I keep mementos in boxes
for you to open when you come back
so the moments return too
that time might try to erase

A photo, a card
you made for your mom
a half-written poem
this unfinished song

A cap, a pennant,
a leaflet, a bulletin,
such dangerous weapons as these
that tore you from me...

And where do I put your smile
if there's no box for the pain
and where do I keep my sadness
when I breathe and sense your fragrance

The insanity of dreaming
the counterculture of thinking
one of those loving wings
that will bring us together again

I keep mementos in boxes...

*[Translations by Jonathan Arries]*

**ELISA LOGAN**
(Tegucigalpa, 1964)

**(NO PHOTOGRAPH, AT THE POET'S REQUEST)**

**A fuego cruzado**

Mañana simularé que aquí,
"No pasa nada".
Otros, pondrán a flor de pecho
su esperanza y caminarán bajo el sol.

A veces,
es necesario fingir demencia
tomar un respiro y
mirar bajo el brillo
de unos desleídos ojos
todo el rumor de acumulados siglos
abalanzarse sobre esta realidad absurda
para poder continuar.

*Febrero del 2010*

**ELISA LOGAN**

Professional name of a poet and theater actress. Master's in Social Work, National Autonomous University (UNAH); degree in Letters and French Pedagogy, Francisco Morazón National Pedagogical University (UPNFM); diplomas in Secondary Education and in Spanish literature; studies in Spain, Germany and Colombia. "A Cuatro Voces" (In Four Voices) Award, 2011. Member of the National Association of Honduran Women Writers (ANDEH). Participant in literary events in Honduras and abroad and in the VIII Latin American and Caribbean Art Teachers Conference (Cuba). Guest of honor, Poets' Conference of Ecuador, 2008. Poems in newspapers, magazines, and anthologies. Published books: *Poemas para un angel caído* (Poems for a Fallen Angel, 1997); *De sueños y realidades* (Of Dreams and Realities, 2001); *Todas y ninguna* (All and None, novel, 2003); *Signos referenciales* (Referential Signs, 2005); *Entre adioses y olvidos* (Between Farewells and Forgetting, 2010).

**In the Crossfire**

Tomorrow I will pretend that
"Nothing's the matter" here.
Others will wear their hope on their sleeve
and walk under the sun.

Sometimes,
you have to feign dementia
take a breath and
look beneath the glare
of fading eyes
how the drone of centuries amassed
leaps onto this absurd reality,
so that you can go on.

*February 2010*

**Viviendo el evangelio**

Padre, le niegan la tierra
madre suya y madre nuestra,
madre de esos bosques
que no lo vieron nacer
pero lo saben amar.

El rumor de los pinos olanchanos
le reclama, Padre;
pide justicia para sus principios
ajustados al evangelio
que yo aspiro a profesar.

Pero su fuerza, Padre,
es sombra benéfica,
invencible resistencia
que contagia.

¡**T**an grande es su amor
**A** este pueblo y esta tierra!
**M**as la avaricia y el poder
**A**rguyen en su contra "patriotismo".
**Y** usted sencillo y noble como es,
**O** les perdona o les absuelve;

Usted decidirá.

    11/9/9

## Living the Gospel

Father, they deny you the Earth,
your mother and our mother
mother of those forests
that did not witness your birth
but know how to love you.

The murmur of the Olancho pines
claims you, Father;
it demands justice for your principles
aligned with the Gospel,
which I aspire to profess.

But your strength, Father,
is a benign shade,
an invisible and
contagious resistance.

Though avarice and power
Argue against you, citing patriotism,
Modest and noble,
And with great love for this people and this land,
You either forgive them
Or absolve them;

You shall decide.

*September 11, 2009*

## Entre adioses y olvidos y la paz...
*"Para los que a pesar de todo, sueñan"*

La niebla violenta de la represión
desvanece la poca paz en que dormíamos.
Retumba la soberbia, retuerce el brazo,
rompe lo que encuentra, ruge,
relincha y repliega con su rabia tenaz.

Y el pueblo resiste.
Con las manos limpias,
con las puras manos
demanda libertad.
Libertad para soñar, vivir, opinar
y volver a reír.

Pero la macana y el fusil no entienden de razones
sólo de muerte y dolor; de orgías brutales.

Ingenua como siempre
sigo soñando con la exiliada paz;
paz para mis hijos
y los hijos de tus hijos
mientras marcho en resistencia
bajo un rancio olor a represión.

## Between Farewells and Forgetting and Peace...
*"To those who dream in spite of it all."*

Repression's violent fog
dispels the scant peace in which we slept.
Pride bellows, twists the arm,
breaks what it finds, roars,
neighs and withdraws with its tenacious fury.

And the people resist.
With clean hands,
with pure hands,
they demand freedom.
Freedom to dream, to live, to speak up,
to laugh again.

But the club and the rifle know no reason,
only death and pain; only brutal orgies.

Naïve as always,
I keep dreaming of our exiled peace;
peace for my children
and your children's children,
as I march in resistance
beneath repression's rancid smell.


*[Translations by Alba F. Aragón]*

## GRECIA LOZANO
### (Puerto de San Lorenzo, Valle, 1993)

**Triste despedida. Hasta luego, Comandante**

Una lágrima cayó.
Un corazón se frustró,
Un alma se envenenó
y la muerte nos atacó.

Un presidente derrocado
una democracia que se quedó a medio palo,
uno y cientos de seres humanos que su vida ofrendaron,
un fantasma que recorre Honduras
ha despertado.

Un sueño congelado,
un vuelo perdido,
un alma hecha pedazos, y
una vida
sin destino.

Un indio se revuelve en su sepulcro,
un hondureño se va de su tierra,
un dictador se ríe en su guarida,
un pueblo entero camina hacia la despedida.

La casa presidencial queda sola,
la embajada de Brasil pierde importancia,
un avión sale del Toncontín,
una nueva historia -con menos esperanza-
comienza desde el fin.
      *(27 de enero de 2010)*

**GRECIA LOZANO**
Law student, National Autonomous University (UNAH). Student delegate from the Law School to the UNAH University Council. National Student Oratory Prize, 2007; National Enterprising Youth Award, 2009; Honduran representative at the First Gathering of Youth of the Americas on Secondary Education, during the meeting of education ministers of member states of the Organization of American States, Quito, Ecuador, 2009. Invited by Brazil's National Student Union to the First Gathering of Latin American and Caribbean Secondary Students, 2009; official delegate to the 17th World Festival of Youth and Students, held in South Africa, 2010. Member of the Political Organization Los Necios-Honduras (OPLN-Honduras).

**A Sad Goodbye. Farewell, *Comandante***

A tear fell.
A heart in frustration grew,
a soul was poisoned
and death attacked us.

A president overthrown
a democracy left undone
one and hundreds of human beings who offered their lives,
a ghost that roams Honduras
has awakened.

A dream frozen,
A flight lost,
a soul shredded to pieces, and
a life
with no destiny.

An Indian stirs in his tomb,
a Honduran leaves his land,
a dictator laughs in his lair,
an entire nation walks toward the farewell.

The presidential house is alone,
the Brazilian embassy loses its importance,
a plane leaves Toncontin,
A new story -with less hope-
begins with the end.
    *(January 27, 2010)*

## El Show del Siglo XXI en Honduras

Eran las 10:56 de la mañana
los medios de comunicación anunciaban su llegada,
el mundo piensa que él no tiene la culpa
de lo que le hicieron los militares de la cúpula.

Decía un periodista vendido
que el Presidente Lobo *"No hará su recorrido"*
que Zelaya era al que *"habíamos corrido"*
y que ojalá tenga en República Dominicana un mejor destino.

Mis lágrimas de juventud cayeron,
se fueron mis sueños rodando por mis mejillas
observaba en la televisión la aglomeración de gente golpista.

No sé si esto es una derrota,
o si es un gran comienzo de revolución
puedo predecir mucha indignación
y espero que el pueblo tome una decisión.

Este es un *show*,
sólo para los invitados.
Esta es la gran burla
para los que por este país
su vida han entregado.

¡Dios, unión y libertad!

*(27 de enero de 2010)*

# The Show of the 21st Century in Honduras

It was 10:56 in the morning
the media were announcing his arrival
the world believes he is not to blame
for what the military at the top did to him.

A sold-out journalist said
President Lobo *"won't dare make inauguration-day rounds"*
Zelaya was the one that *"we chased away"*
and we wish him better luck in the Dominican Republic.

My youthful tears fell,
my dreams rolled down my cheeks
I saw on TV the agglomeration of *golpistas*.

I don't know if this is a defeat,
Or if it's the great beginning of a revolution
I can predict much indignation
and I hope the nation will make a decision.

This is a show,
only for those invited.
This is the big joke
for those who have given their lives
for this country.

God, unity and freedom!

*(January 27, 2010)*

**Libre**

La libertad es voluntad,
Independientemente de nada y todo,
Buscá encasillar la vida como un preciado tesoro
Refundar lo que existe mientras en la
Espera se detiene el pueblo que resiste.

La libertad es objetivamente abstracta
Irónica en medio de un sistema opresor
Brillante diamante en la juventud
Rescatada de las cenizas de la
Esperanza y sus rincones infinitos.

Llorás amigo/a mío/a, pero
Inevitablemente así como te indignás así debés luchar
Burlando este sistema de nuestra sociedad
Resumiendo en actos tu penar y pensar,
Emigrando hacia el amor a la humanidad.

Proclamá conmigo la canción de la libertad y refundación,
imaginá que no hay sobre la Honduras una vía mejor,
que sobre el mar y bajo el cielo
te permita descansar y tirar tus cadenas de esclavitud al
alta mar.

Sé libre amigo/a mío/a,
sé libre,
y luchá por el amor que merecés,
por la libertad que creés merecer.

*(27 de junio de 2012)*

## Libre-Free*

Liberty is willingness,
Independently of nothing and everything,
By guarding life like a precious treasure
Refounding what already exists while
Ever the resisting nation awaits.

Liberty is objectively abstract
Ironic in the midst of an oppressive system
Brilliant diamond for youth
Rescued from the ashes of
Everlasting hope and its infinite corners.

Let yourself cry, my friend, but
Inevitably, as you grow indignant, so should you fight
By outwitting this system in our society
Revealing in acts your pain and thought,
Emigrating toward love for humanity.

Proclaim with me the song of liberty and refounding,
imagine that for Honduras there is no better path
that on the sea and under the sky
would allow you to rest and throw your slave shackles
into the deep sea.

Be free, my friend,
be free,
and fight for the love you deserve,
for the liberty you believe you deserve.

    (June 27, 2012)


*[Translations by Marie Pfaff]*

---

* The first letters of the verses in the first three stanzas spell "LIBRE," FREE. This is also the abbreviated name of the political party founded by deposed president Manuel Zelaya Rosales, the Liberty and Refounding Party

## WALDINA MEJÍA MEDINA
### (Tegucigalpa, 1963)

**Poema para Isy con Honduras**
    *En honra de Isy Obed Murillo Mencía, de 19 años.*
    *Asesinado el 5 de julio del 2009 por militares que dispararon a los manifestantes contra el golpe militar-diputadil en Honduras del 28 de junio, y la restitución del Presidente electo. En honra de tantos compañeros asesinados/as en esta lucha.*
    *Su padre declaró:*
    *"...nos duele su muerte, pero me siento orgulloso que no muere por delincuen¬te, ni por borracho, sino por las causas que nos han reprimido".*

    NO hay modo
no hay ninguna manera de expresar
el dolor más cortante
la furia más eterna.
NO hay modo, no hay razones,
sólo este llanto negro que nos hierve en el pecho
que se agolpa gritando con doscientas mil voces
por este hijo nuestro
asesinado.

# WALDINA MEJÍA MEDINA

Also uses "Waldina Medina" as her literary name. Degree in Linguistics and Educational Guidance, Francisco Morazán National Pedagogical University (UPNFM), and Master's in Central American Literature, National Autonomous University (UNAH). Member of the National Association of Honduran Women Writers (ANDEH). Organizer with Armida García and Raynier Alfaro of the international poetry festival, The Dissidents' Turn. Selected for a number of national and international anthologies. Participant in literary gatherings and symposiums in several countries, including the United States, Mexico, Ecuador, Peru, Brazil, Costa Rica, El Salvador, Panama, Puerto Rico and Germany. Published works: *El amor y sus iras* (Love and Its Rages, 2001); *Catorce sonetos con estrambote* (Fourteen Sonnets with Strambotto, 2002); *Poemas de Gustavo* (Poems for Gustavo, 2010); *La Tía Sofi y los otros cuentos* (Aunt Sofi and Other Stories, 2002).

## Poem for Isy, for Honduras

*In honor of Isy Obed Murillo Mencía, age 19.*
*Killed on July 15, 2009, by soldiers who fired on demonstrators protesting the military- congressional coup in Honduras of June 28 and demanding the reinstatement of the elected president. In honor of the many compañeros killed in this struggle.*
*His father stated:*
*". . . his death is painful for us, but I am proud that he did not die as a delinquent or a drunk, but fighting the causes of our repression."*

    NO way
there is no way to express
the sharpest pain
the most eternal fury.
NO way, there are no reasons,
only this black cry that boils in the chest
that pounds screaming with two hundred thousand voices
for this son of ours
murdered.

    Un hijo que nos costó crecer
con los ojos abiertos, muy abiertos
hacia la humanidad,
    que no llegaba a veinte años
    pero que acumulaba
siglos y siglos de aleteantes
esperanzas y sueños
por justicia y equidad y una vida digna
a todas las personas, aún la más débil y sencilla.
    Un hijo con el pecho luminoso
como aquél, como ella
como tantos y miles
que luchan por verdadera democracia.
    Un hijo que no murió como un borracho, un ladrón
                  y menos
un corrupto
sino como un valiente luchador del pueblo.
    Un hijo y una bala y un francotirador.
En las filas cerradas de soldados
que atacaban
las filas abiertas y sin armas de doscientos mil manifestantes
en contra de otro golpe militar
    el francotirador buscando entre las ráfagas del odio
    un blanco fácil
    apuntó sin dudar
    al hijo nuestro
    y le cerró los ojos llenos de humanidad
y le abrió la cabeza
y escaparon aleteando con fuerza
sus inmortales sueños
y el dolor y la furia como abono
para sembrarse aún más entre los pechos
de la multitud que aquí quedamos.
    Cayó su cuerpo entre su sangre y sesos.
¡Asesinos, asesinos, asesinos!
gritamos impotentes y furiosos
levantando los puños y los pechos.
    Un muerto es demasiado
y ya son muchos, Honduras, tus muertos
para salvarte de tus secuestradores

      A son we labored to raise
with his eyes open, very open
toward humanity,
      who was not yet 20
      but who had gathered
centuries and centuries of passionate
hopes and dreams
of justice and equality and a life of dignity
for all, even the weakest and most humble.
      A son with a radiant heart
like the others, like him, like her
like the thousands
who fight for true democracy.
      A son who didn't die a drunkard or a thief
certainly not corrupt
he died a brave defender of the people.
      A son, a bullet, a sniper.
In the closed ranks of soldiers
who attacked
the open unarmed ranks of two hundred thousand demonstrating
against another military coup
      the sniper searching among the waves of hate
      for an easy target
      aimed without hesitation
      at our son
      and closed his eyes full of humanity
and tore open his head
and his immortal dreams
and the pain and rage
escaped with beating wings to feed,
to plant themselves in the hearts
of the many who remain.
      His body fell, blood and brains.
Murderers! Murderers! Murderers!
we screamed impotent and furious
our fists raised, our bearing proud.
      One death is too many
and yours, Honduras, are so many that
you cannot be saved from your kidnappers

que te esquilman y hacen morir de hambre
a la gran mayoría de tu pueblo,
golpistas del Estado cada vez que no les cuadra
su democracia de vitrina.
  ¡Asesinos, asesinos, asesinos!
  Y NO hay modo, no hay forma de decir
este eterno dolor
que nos abisma, que nos enardece
por este hijo nuestro asesinado
por este hermano, hijo y padre nuestro
del cielo aquí en la Tierra.

who hold you hostage and let
your people die of hunger
who attack the State whenever
its false democracy becomes inconvenient to them.
  Murderers! Murderers! Murderers!
  And NO way, there is no way to tell of
this endless pain
that drowns us, that consumes us
for this our murdered son
for this brother, son and our father
in heaven here on Earth.

*[Translation by Janet N. Gold]*

# VENUS IXCHEL MEJÍA
## (Tegucigalpa, 1979)

**¿Dónde está la democracia?**

Dijeron
mientras la buscaban tras las caries del pueblo
con la inspección obtusa del fusil.

Entraron a la casa
con el desenfado de las retinas
y su jubilosa agnosia en la tv.
No supimos qué decirles,
la luz siempre nos abandona
justo a las puertas
de la factura vencida de la noche.

"Acá no ha venido"
es lo único que alcanzamos a decir
mientras poníamos resistencia
con las manos detrás de la nuca.
"Se lo juro señor militar, acá no la hemos visto"
apenas balbuceábamos
con el aire apretado después del golpe.

# VENUS IXCHEL MEJÍA

Poet, editor, cultural activist and promoter. Musical Education degree, National School of Music, 1997. Degree in Letters, National Autonomous University (UNAH), 2006. Participant in artistic and cultural activities, including national events and the Olanchito, Yoro, Juegos Florales, 2000-2001; I International Poetry Festival in Nahuat Pipil Land, El Salvador, 2013; II Encounter of Women Poets, Papaloapan Basin, Mexico, 2014. Producer and host of the cultural-literary radio program "Molinos de Viento" (Windmills), National Radio of Honduras, 2005-2006. Leader of literary workshops, including the "Barrio Lindo" (Pretty Neighborhood) project sponsored by the President's Office. Cofounder and editor, Editorial Ixchel, since 2011. Publications: poetry, *Ad Líbitum* (Editorial Ixchel, 2012); poetry anthology, *Lírica de vida* (Life Lyric, Signum Editors, 2012); anthology of the II Encounter of Women Poets, Papaloapan Basin, Mexico, *Soles de media noche* (Midnight Suns, 2014).

## Where is Democracy?

They said
as they searched in the cavities of the people
obtusely performing an armed inspection.

They entered the house
with boldness in their retinas
and jubilant agnosia on the TV.
We didn't know what to tell them
light always abandons us
right at the gates
of night's past-due bill.

"It hasn't come here"
is all we managed to say
as we resisted
with our hands behind our necks.
"I swear, Mr. Soldier, we haven't seen it here"
we barely mumbled
with short breath, after the coup.

La democracia es desde entonces
un fugitivo,
un holograma de computadora
protagonista del reality show
para sobrellevar su ausencia.

Quizá aún la veamos en la tinta de la renuncia adulterada
en las manos alzadas del congreso recién lavadas de la
última masturbación con el empréstito de turno
en la voz en off de la ninfómana cadena nacional
en el toque de queda de la historia
escondida bajo nuestros dedos apretados
cansados de ser puño,
puños que soñaron ser
un golpe de justicia.

Democracy since then is
a fugitive,
a computer-generated hologram
star of the reality show
to survive its absence.

Perhaps we will see it in the ink of the adulterated resignation
in Congress's raised hands, recently washed after the
latest masturbation with the newest official loan
in the off-screen voice of the nymphomaniacal national
                                            broadcast network
in the curfew on history
hidden under our clenched fingers
tired of being fisted,
fists that dreamed of being
a blow for justice.

## Sin Reproche

Te doy
Honduras
mis ojos
para llorar contigo
mi boca
para cantarte
y besar tus heridas
mis sueños
para nunca verte
derrotada
mis brazos
para sujetarte
y sostenerte
cuando te derribe la infamia
mis pasos para marchar contigo
aunque todo parezca irrevocable
mis alas de bronce
mi pecho de lata
mis acordes de anhelo
para no olvidarte
Honduras
todo
te lo doy sin reproche
menos mi vida
porque esa
quiero vivirla todavía...

**Without Reproach**

I give you
Honduras
my eyes
to cry with you
my mouth
to sing to you
and kiss your wounds
my dreams
to never see you
defeated
my arms
to hold you
and support you
when infamy knocks you down
my steps to march with you
although all may seem irrevocable
my wings of bronze
my chest of tin
my chords of desire
to not forget you
Honduras
everything
I give all to you without reproach
except my life
because that
I still want to live...

**Resistencia**

Mi cabeza
hoy está poblada
de un ejército de sueños,
sueños de justicia.

La infamia
es el buitre que despedaza
el famélico vientre de mi patria.
De sur a norte voces se elevan,
incendiarias pancartas
son palomas pintadas
con sangre embravecida,
la bandera ondea herida
ahí donde están blandiendo
el arma homicida.

Yo quiero salir
y aunque ellos tienen la bandera
yo tengo el puño alzado
que ahora nos representa
la boca contraída, la camisa negra.
Siento el calor de la lid
en la sangre que me abrasa
estoy lista para la marcha sin retorno.

Pero vos estás a mi lado.
En tu boca poblada de poesía
está mi alegría,
querés que la cama
sea la trinchera
donde dibujemos un destino
más feliz que este harapo de historia
que hemos tenido,
que los besos incendiarios
despierten las revoluciones de nuestros cuerpos fríos.

No obstante mi lugar es allá
hombro a hombro en la lucha,

**Resistence**

My head
today is populated
with an army of dreams,
dreams of justice.

Infamy
is the vulture that rips apart
the famished belly of my homeland.
From south to north voices rise,
inflammatory banners
are doves painted
with raging blood,
the flag flutters wounded
there where they brandish
the murderous gun.

I want to go out
and though they have the flag
I have the raised fist
that now represents us
the contorted mouth, the black shirt.
I feel the heat of the battle
in the blood that's boiling in me
I'm ready for the march of no return.

But you are at my side.
In your mouth filled with poetry
is my happiness,
you want our bed
to be the trench
where we design a destiny
happier than this shred of history
that we have had,
where incendiary kisses
awaken revolutions in our cold bodies

However, my place is there
shoulder to shoulder in the struggle,

en medio del clamor popular
y la agonía del miedo,
y vos me llamás
a que mis sueños aniden a tu lado,
donde, después del accésit del amor,
el verso sea la patria que canta.

in midst of the popular outcry
and agonizing fear,
and you call me
for my dreams to nest at your side,
where, after love's futile attempt,
verse will be the homeland that sings.

*[Translations by Christopher Potts]*

# FANNY MELÉNDEZ
## (Catacamas, Olancho, 1971)

**Otro golpe**

Otro golpe,
otro dolor,
que da a luz
lo no nacido
del amor.

Porque el amor se escapó
de los cuerpos de todos.
Sólo quedaron los restos andantes,
sepulcros ambulantes, vísceras secas,
llenas de odio, que detrás de una sonrisa
hincan sus feroces dientes sobre el cuello
confiado del otro.
Son viles y serviles para mantener su status quo,
matan un ave y se sienten culpables,
sin embargo, día a día, metódicamente
matan el pan no diario de la mesa.
Día a día, metódicamente
saquean la exigua arca de todos,
tratan de robar la sonrisa de un niño,
asedian la esperanza del hombre y la mujer
fornican con la honestidad del pueblo,
trafican con el derecho de ser sano y educado.
Por eso, los ojos del cielo se cerraron
porque la tierra se tiñó de rojo tinto
que enceguecía hasta la mirada del hombre
más perverso.

**FANNY MELÉNDEZ**

Degrees in Letters, National Pedagogical University Francisco Morazán (UPNFM) and National Autonomous University (UNAH); Master's in Educational Communication and Technologies, Latin American Institute of Educational Communication (México-Honduras). Professor in the Department of Letters, UNAH. Presentations at academic conferences in Honduras and abroad. Publications: "*Esfinge y Ariel*, dos revistas de Froylán Turcios," in the virtual magazine *Istmo*, and poems in *Revista Ixbalam*. Contributor to Juan Antonio Hormigón's *Biografía cronológica y epistolario de Valle Inclán, Volume II*, on Valle Inclán's collaboration in *Esfinge* and *Ariel*. Unpublished works: "Rubén Berríos, Analysis of His Work" and the poetry collection *Cicatrices, (Scars)*.

**Another Blow**

Another blow,
another pain
birthing
what is not born
of love.

Because love left
everyone's bodies.
All that is left are the walking remains,
traveling graves, dry guts
full of hate which, behind a smile,
thrust ferocious teeth into
the other's trusting neck.
They are vile and servile to maintain their status quo,
they kill a bird and feel guilty,
yet, day by day, methodically,
they kill our not-so-daily bread.
Day by day, methodically,
they loot everyone's meager treasure,
they try to steal a child's smile,
they hound the hope of men and women,
they fornicate with the people's honesty,
they traffic in the right to be schooled and healthy.
That is why heaven's eyes closed
for the Earth was stained a dark red
that blinded even the gaze
of the most perverse man.

**Yo soy todas, todos y una**

Yo soy todas, todos y una
vivo en mí el amor, el dolor, la alegría
de muchas, de muchos; soy un país sangrante
Es la fiesta del dolor compartida,
la casa lóbrega del desamor,
la cama desabrida del egoísmo,
la mesa insípida de los viles serviles,
la constante huida de la más efímera
sonrisa.

Siento la algarabía del dolor en mi carne,
en mis huesos, en mí se aúna y acuna el amor,
el dolor, la alegría de todas , de todos en una suerte
de mímesis que troca en rojo las calles, las casas,
el campo y la ciudad.

Yo soy todas, todos y una.
Quisiera ser un país floreciente,
lleno de rosas rojas, pero no de sangre,
lleno de sonrisas sinceras y fuertes, pero no de zalamería,
lleno de certezas, donde la niña, el niño se hagan viejos, /
      pero no el homicidio, femicidio...
lleno de confianza, optimismo, respeto y honestidad
que son frutos del amor.

## I Am All Women, All Men, and One

I am all women, all men, and one
I live, in me, the love, the pain, the joy
of many women, many men; I am a bleeding country.
This is the shared feast of pain,
the dreary house of lovelessness,
the crude bed of egoism,
the bland table of the vile and servile,
the constant escape of even the most ephemeral
smile.

I feel the jubilation of pain in my flesh,
in my bones, love gathers and curls up inside me,
together with the pain, the joy of all women, all men,
                                                    in a sort
of mimesis in which streets, houses,
countryside and city turn red.

I am all women, all men, and one.
I would like to be a flowering country,
full of red roses, but not blood,
full of strong and true smiles, but not flattery,
full of certainties, where the girl, the boy, can grow old,/
        but not homicide, femicide...
full of trust, optimism, respect, and honesty
which are the fruits of love.

## Piensan que se llevarán todo al morir

Piensan que se llevarán todo al morir
piensan que andarán para siempre
en sus carros último modelo,
en sus casas de revista internacional,
en sus villas de campo y retiro,
en sus finanzas en el extranjero con sus crecidas cuentas,
en sus paseos de placer fuera del país
en fin, en todas las "bondades" que el dinero da.

Piensan que hasta su cuarta o quinta generación
sus hijas, sus hijos tendrán asegurada
la sonrisa perfecta, el estar bien
la educación en el extranjero,
la salud de los hospitales fuera de las fronteras,
el puesto alto dentro del engranaje del gobierno,
la disposición servil de un pueblo sentenciado por
el hambre, la desprotección e impotencia.

Todas, todos, yo o quizá algunos pensamos,
que no está bien que tengan tanto,
si no comparten con otros,
que si todas, todos, tienen suficiente, una mesa ataviada
de pan y bebida, una casa digna, no hacinada, una cama
bien acolchonada, una educación esmerada y la salud bien
compensada, todas, todos, sin excepción, tendrán
        asegurada la alegría
de un buen vivir, sin el asedio de la violencia, de la impunidad,
de la presencia del terrible designio de la miseria y su querida
hermana Paupérrima.

## They Think They'll Take It All With Them When They Die

They think they'll take it all with them when they die,
they think they'll live forever
with their latest-model cars,
with their international-magazine homes,
with their country villas and retirement,
with their swollen accounts and finances abroad,
with their pleasure trips outside the country,
in short, with all the "comforts" money grants.

They think that up to the fourth or fifth generation
their daughters, their sons, will find assured
the perfect smile, their well-being,
their education abroad,
the care of hospitals outside our borders,
the high post in the government's machinery
the servile disposition of a people sentenced by
hunger, defenselessness and impotence.

All women, all men, I, or maybe some of us, think
it is not right for them to have so much
if they do not share with others,
that if all women, all men, have enough, a table dressed
with bread and drink, a respectable home, not overcrowded, a bed
that is well cushioned, a thorough education, and health
well taken care of, then all women, all men, without
                              exception, will have
       the joy
of a good life assured, without the hounding of violence, of impunity,
of misery's terrible plans and of its dear
sister, Indigence.

*[Translations by Alba F. Aragón]*

# IRIS MENCÍA BÁRCENAS
## (Tegucigalpa, 1959)

**Nada pasa**

Nada ha pasado aquí
todo está bien
sólo esa veloz carrera de veloces piernas
y cuerpos pintados de sangre
y púrpura de gases
nada es
en la inveterada costumbre
del sol que amanece con las calles sucias
y las paredes escritas.
Nada ha pasado
Sólo el alma que se escapa por la boca del dolor
y los golpes
y la ira y el poder en la atmósfera
entre los pasos perdidos de cien/ doscientos/
quinientos mil hombres y mujeres
con el agitado corazón en la mano
y en los ojos el brillo de un mar innombrable
en este país de apariencias
donde los espejos son los escudos militares.

## IRIS MENCÍA BÁRCENAS

Journalist, fiction writer, and poet. Winner of the UNICEF Press Award. Broadcaster for 16 years with Radio America. Member of the National Association of Honduran Women Writers (ANDEH). Participant in: May celebration, Las Romerías de Mayo, in Holguín, Cuba; Meeting of Caribbean Writers, Chetumal, Mexico; and other regional literary events. She left her country in 1999 for Costa Rica and returned months later to publish *La máscara del despojo* (The Mask of Plunder, 1999), a controversial book on corruption. Other publications: *Hojas sueltas* (Loose Pages, 2004); *Desde adentro* (From Within, 2011); *Golpes sin olvido* (Unforgetting Blows/Coups, 2012); *Recuerdos habitados* (Inhabited Memories, 2012).

### Nothing's Happening[*]

Nothing has happened here
everything is fine
only that swift race of swift legs
and bodies painted in blood
and the purple of gases
nothing is
in the c ommon habit
of the sun that dawns on dirty streets
and graffitied walls.
Nothing has happened
only the soul that escapes through the pained mouth
and the blows
and the rage and the power in the atmosphere
between the lost steps of one hundred/two hundred/
five hundred thousand men and women
with their agitated hearts in their hands
and in their eyes the gleam of an unnamable sea
in this country of appearances
where mirrors are military shields.

---

[*] Reference to official government statements during repression and resistance that there was no cause for alarm because, "Nothing is happening here."

## Tinta y sangre (Elecciones espurias, Honduras 2009)

No puedo llegar hasta esos lugares
algo impide recorrer el camino
donde el humanismo se pierde.
El corazón lo impide, lo impide la columna,
tampoco la rodilla y menos aún
este pie testarudo quiere llegar hasta las urnas.
Y es que entrar a esos lugares de tintas indelebles
que se borran al guiño de un ojo,
sería echar en saco roto la roja sangre patria
Matria fragmentada;
sería esparcir el humo asesino
que contamina el canto de las montañas
y aleja nuevos amaneceres,
sería traicionarse
morirse de vergüenza.
No. No hay manera posible de dejar la huella
en el golpe y sus crímenes.

## Ink and Blood (False Elections, Honduras, 2009)

I cannot reach those places
something impedes my traveling the road
where humanism is lost.
The heart impedes it, the spine impedes it,
not the knee and even less
this stubborn foot wants to get to the ballot box.
And it's that entering those places of indelible ink
that gets erased in the wink of an eye,
would be to toss into a torn sack the country's red blood
Motherland fragmented;
it would be to spread the murderous smoke
that contaminates the song of the mountains
and distances new dawns,
it would be to betray oneself
to die of shame.
No. There is no possible way to leave a trace
in the coup and its crimes.

**Estado del tiempo**

Escandalosas chicharras
cantan o quizá lloran
a un cielo que no llueve.
El oído se aguza y la vista recuerda
la amenaza es saltar al llanto.
Los escudos militares
irritan los ojos-
los silbidos de balas
son hilos de sangre que se abrazan a la tierra
mientras las máscaras caen
los rostros se descubren y el sol les duele
entonces se agazapan
dan zarpazos
y ese es el estado del tiempo
en este tiempo de golpe.

**State of Time**

Scandalous cicadas
sing or perhaps they cry
to a sky that does not rain.
Hearing sharpens and eyes remember
the threat is breaking into tears.
The military shields
irritate the eyes-
the whistling of the bullets
are threads of blood that embrace the earth
while masks fall off
faces are uncovered and the sun hurts them
then they crouch down
and run off
and that is the state of time
in this time of the coup.*


*[Translations by Joan F. Marx]*

---

* Note the play on the term in Spanish for coup d´état, "golpe de estado" literally, a strike of blow against the State, here changed to "state of time" and "this time of the coup".

## MELISSA MERLO
### (Danlí, El Paraíso, 1969)

**El amor es...**

...es una madreselva que florece
en la noche de la muerte
abonada por el amor derramado
en la sangre de un joven
que espera en el infinito la justicia.

...es un destello de vida
que se apaga en cualquier tiempo
arrebatado por el patrono del crimen
que impune deambula por Honduras
sembrando jóvenes en el valle de la muerte.

...es una delicada gota de rocío
que nace en la mañana
y desaparece con el sol de la tragedia
que calcina la tersa piel de una muchacha
borrando las huellas del ultraje.

# MELISSA MERLO

Poet, fiction writer, essayist. Bachelor's degree, Francisco Morazán National Pedagogical University (UPNFM); Master's in Education, University of Lincoln-Nebraska. Professor and Research Coordinator, University Distance Education Center, UPNFM. Member, Union of Writers and Artists of Honduras (UEAH); Editorial Director of Verbo Editores. Radio and television producer and presenter for cultural and entertainment programming. Published works: *Color Cristal* (Color of Glass, poetry, 2007); coeditor of *Poesía hondureña en resistencia* (Honduran Poetry in Resistance, 2009); *Honduras sendero en resistencia* (Honduras Path in Resistance, 2010); and *Antología del cuento hondureño siglo XXI* (Anthology of 21st-Century Short Stories in Honduras, 2012). Email: melymerlo@yahoo.com.

## Love Is...

...it is a honeysuckle that blooms
during the night of death
fertilized by love spilled
in the blood of a youth
who awaits justice in the infinite.

...it is a twinkle of life
that burns out at any time
yanked away by the master of crime
who wanders unpunished through Honduras
sowing youths in the valley of death.

...it is a delicate drop of dew
that is born in the morning
and disappears with the sun of tragedy
that chars the smooth skin of a girl
erasing the marks of attack.

... es una cara al suelo salpicada de rojo
... es un hijo que no saldrá del vientre
... es un cordel furioso en el cuello
... es un machete que aniquila la esperanza

... es una madre que surca los vientos
en vana busca del alma de sus hijos
que desde lo etéreo la llaman
sin comprender sus lágrimas.

... it is a face to the ground spattered with blood
... it is a child who will not leave the womb
... it is a furious cord around the neck
... it is a machete that annihilates hope.

... it is a mother that ploughs the winds
searching in vain for the souls of her children
who call her from ethereal space
without understanding her tears.

## Espejo mágico

*¿Quién es la más linda?*

Miro manchas azules
en tu rostro de furia.
Mejillas y nudillos
en la misma sombra.
Lunares de piel desnuda
en tu cráneo de estela maya.
*¿Espejito... quién es la más linda?*
Veo en tus pechos
huellas de dientes ajenos.
Hombros y brazos
dislocados por la misma soga.
Sobras de pútrido semen
en tus caderas de piedra.
*¿Espejito, espejito mágico...?*
Descubro tu vientre revolucionario
invadido a fuerza bruta
falos de carne y de madera
golpes de vientre
golpes de alma.
Muere la mujer.
Vive la patria.

## Magic Mirror

*Who's the fairest of them all?*

I look at the blue stains
on your furious face.
Cheeks and knuckles
in the same shadow.
Bald patches
on your Mayan stele-like skull.
*Mirror, mirror on the wall, who's the fairest of them all?*
On your breasts I see
someone's teeth marks.
Shoulders and arms
dislocated by the same rope.
Excesses of rotten semen
on your stone hips.
*Mirror mirror, magic mirror...?*
I discover your revolutionary womb
invaded with brute force
phalluses of flesh and wood
blows to the womb
blows to the soul.
The woman dies.
The fatherland lives.

**Ignorantia**

Vive la ignorancia
teñida de colores en
las butacas del Congreso.
Camina altanera
en los pasillos de la Corte.
Duerme en las sábanas
de los rojiblancos.
Baña su cuerpo
en babas de cobras y tigres.
Corta sus uñas
en cajas registradoras.
Su cabello tiñe
en el salón de los golpistas.
El pueblo la espolea
en danza peligrosa
al borde del abismo.

**Ignorantia**

Ignorance lives
bathed in colors on
the seats of Congress.
It walks haughtily
in the halls of the Supreme Court.
It sleeps in the sheets
of the red & whites.*
It bathes its body
in the drool of cobras and tigers.
It cuts its nails
in cash registers.
It dyes its hair
in the salon of the *golpistas*.
The people spur it on
in a dangerous dance
at the edge of the abyss.


*[Translations by Stephanie Saunders]*

---

* Reference to the colors of deposed president Zelaya's Liberal Party flag. Many Liberal Party members were considered *golpistas* because of their complicity in the overthrow of Zelaya.

## MARÍA TOMASA "TOMY" MORALES CASTILLO
### (Tegucigalpa, 1977)

**Héroe anónimo**
*(Dedicado a nuestro querido Edy)*

Allí estaba él
alto, fuerte, imponente,
con su pelo largo en una trenza,
una camiseta sin mangas, ceñida
dejaba ver sus tatuajes,
sus piernas firmes como columnas,
su pecho como de acero,
él siempre al frente de la batalla,
mientras la gente corría para todos lados
él devolvía las bombas
como un experto jugador olímpico,
se subía a las tanquetas para que otros escaparan
de los toletes de los uniformados,
a veces usaba una bandera de túnica,
serio pero en ocasiones sonreía,
se miraba su silueta en medio del humo,
casi pierde un oído por los golpes
de unos gorilas, pero ahí está;
han pasado los años
y él sigue ahí, como un guerrero anónimo,
visible e invisible a la vez.

## MARÍA TOMASA "TOMY" MORALES CASTILLO

Journalist, advocate for Human Rights, Law student at the National Autonomous University (UNAH), militant in the University Reform Front (FRU), the National Popular Resistance Front (FNRP), and the LIBRE Party. Communication contributor at the Tegucigalpa office of the Honduras-Cuba Friendship Association (Asociación de Amistad Honduras Cuba) and the organization of Mesoamerican Women in Resistance for a Life of Dignity (Mesoamericanas en Resistencia por una Vida Digna). Writer of poetry since age 14, mainly based on lived experiences, romantic at first, but later evolving toward realistic and some erotic poetry.


**Anonymous Hero**
  *(Dedicated to our dear Edy)*

There he was
tall, strong, imposing,
with his long hair in a braid,
a sleeveless shirt, tight-fitting
revealed his tattoos,
his legs firm as pillars,
his chest like steel,
always at the battlefront,
while people went running in all directions
he returned the bombs
like an expert Olympic player,
he climbed on tanks so that others could escape
from the soldiers' cudgels,
at times he wrapped himself in a flag,
serious but on occasions he smiled,
you could see his silhouette in the midst of the smoke,
he almost lost his hearing from the blows
of some gorillas, but there he is;
the years have passed
and he's still there, like an anonymous warrior
visible and invisible all at once.

**Ni perdón, ni olvido**

El 28 de junio florecen los sentimientos
de los descalzos, de los desposeídos, de los revolucionarios,
un día como este millones salieron a las calles
por sus ideales de un mundo mejor,
defendiendo a costa de sus vidas
su patria, su presidente, su dignidad,
hombres, mujeres, jóvenes y niños
caminaron al son de los sonetos
que inspiran la valentía
de un pueblo que despierta
de su ensueño de un mundo utópico,
sufrieron la ira de la impotencia
al probar los gases lacrimógenos
los toletes de los militares
y la condenación del religioso amor de las iglesias,
vienen a nuestras mentes
los rostros de las y los compas
que lucharon a nuestro lado
los que creyeron en un mundo mejor
y ofrendaron su sangre como semillas
para la libertad de las futuras generaciones,
quedaron sus gritos, sus risas y anhelos
como inspiración etérea a los corazones
que quedaron luchando con gallardía.
Ni olvido, ni perdón
es el homenaje que les damos
a los mártires de la resistencia,
del Jute, de la huelga del 54,
de las mujeres, los maestros, campesinos,
periodistas, abogados, LGTBI, jóvenes y niños hondureños.

## Neither Forgiving, Nor Forgetting

On the 28th of June feelings spring
from the barefoot, from the dispossessed, from the revolutionaries,
on a day like this millions poured into the streets
for their ideals of a better world,
defending at the cost of their lives
their homeland, their president, their dignity,
men, women, young people and children
marched to the sound of the sonnets
that inspire the bravery
of a people that awakens
from its fantasy of a utopian world,
they suffered the rage of impotence
when they felt the tear gases
the military's cudgels
and condemnation by the religious love of churches,
faces of women and men comrades
who fought by our side
come into our minds
those who believed in a better world
and offered their blood as seeds
for the freedom of future generations,
their cries, their laughter and their dreams remained
as ethereal inspiration to the hearts
that remained fighting with bravery.
Neither forgetting, nor forgiving
is the tribute we offer to them
the martyrs of resistance,
from El Jute, from the strike of 54,
the women, the teachers, farmers
journalists, lawyers, LGTBI, Honduran youth and children.

*[Translations by Kathleen Cunniffe]*

## MAYRA OYUELA
(Tegucigalpa, 1982)

**Cumplir 27**
*A Roque Dalton*

Por esos días, en que la tierra giró alrededor de sí misma,
inagotable, buscando un mejor rostro entre los humanos,
con las manos de frente y de cara al sol, el poder de la palabra
el vicio de dominar los lenguajes húmedos de las piedras.
Ahora entiendo cómo es que se tortura a un hombre, a una mujer.
Ahora entiendo cómo se arrebata la vida,
cómo la serpiente de la guerra de clases
engulle las palabras de la historia, para luego vomitar
con el mismo desdén, la frialdad, las balas que atraviesan continentes,
cercos, ciudades y montañas.
Nada más cruel que sentarse a ver cumplir 27 años, Roque
ahora sé cómo es que un poeta amanece tiritando la angustia
con un fusil en las manos.

Ahora sé qué es odiar a un humano viciado, a un traidor.
Ahora sé, cómo se obtiene una patria.

# MAYRA OYUELA

Poet and cultural activist. Cofounder of the groups País-Poesible and Artists in Resistance, a political and cultural organization made up of cultural workers dedicated to the power of the people and the construction of socialism; its slogan: "Artists armed with culture against barbarity!" Producer of ERGO SUM, a space devoted to music and culture at the Spanish Cultural Center in Tegucigalpa (CCET). Author of *Escribiéndole una casa al barco* (Writing a House for the Boat, 2006) and *Puertos de arribo* (Ports of Entry, 2009).


**Turning 27**
*For Roque Dalton*

In those days, when the earth turned and turned,
unwilling to give up, searching for a better human face,
hands and face to the sun, the power of the word
the hunger to speak the damp languages of stones.
Now I understand what it means to torture a man, or a woman.
Now I understand how life explodes in fury,
how the serpent of class warfare
swallows the words of history, then vomits
with the same frigid disdain, the bullets that cross continents,
walls, cities and mountains.
Nothing is more cruel, Roque, than sitting here turning 27
now I know what it is for a poet to wake up trembling, anguished
with a gun in her hands.

Now I know what it is to hate a corrupt human being, a traitor.
Now I know, how to become a country.

**Nos compromete el grito
(o panfleto descarado)**

Buenos días sindicatos, buenos días socialistas,
trotskistas y seguidores de Gramsci.
Buenos días populistas y proletariado.
Buenos días campesinos, buenos días campesinas,
científicos, intelectuales, líderes, zapateros, ebanistas y poetas.
Buenos días amas de casa, anarquistas,
historiadores, niños, niñas,
marxistas, emos y punks.
Buenos días dramaturgos, actores, músicos, y orejas.
Buenos días docentes, artistas
estudiantes, feministas, taxistas
escultores, camareros e incrédulos.
Bienvenidas ratas, bienvenido sol,
bienvenida piedra, zanates, seudo derechos humanos
garrotes e infiltrados:
Estamos todos reunidos hoy aquí
porque en casa presidencial
amaneció gobernando una cucaracha.
Camaradas puristas del lenguaje,
no pediré disculpas por el panfleto
porque desde los estercoleros de New York
se promueve la sangre,
residimos en el lugar que habita el hombre,
convivimos en el lugar donde lapidan al hombre a la mujer
y no queremos más hijos para llorar.
Nos compromete el grito,
nos compromete la luz que se dispara
desde los fusiles de nuestras gargantas
desde la apostura de sabernos todos hijos e hijas de la carne,
dioses y diosas de carne.
Pedimos pan y nos dan hambre,
pedimos respeto y nos proveen soborno.
No doblaremos las rodillas,
no es tiempo de orar.
No esperaremos que crucifiquen nuestra opinión

## Our Voice Raised in Protest Obligates Us
## (or Shameless Rhetoric)

Good morning unions, good morning socialists,
Trotskyists and followers of Gramsci.
Good morning populists and proletariat.
Good morning men and women who work the land,
scientists, intellectuals, leaders, shoemakers, carpenters
                                                          and poets.
Good morning housewives, anarchists,
historians, boys, girls,
Marxists, emos and punks.
Good morning playwrights, actors, musicians and informers.
Good morning teachers, artists
students, feminists, cab drivers
sculptors, waiters and skeptics.
Welcome rats, welcome sun,
welcome stone, grackles, pseudo human rights
cudgels and stool pigeons:
We are gathered together here today
because as of this morning a cockroach
governs in the presidential palace.
Comrades who are language purists,
I make no excuses for my rhetoric
because the cesspools of New York
have incited bloodshed,
we reside in the place inhabited by man,
we live in the place where men and women are stoned to death
and we don't want more children to weep over.
Our voice raised in protest obligates us,
the light obligates us shot
from the guns of our throats
from the courage of knowing we are all sons and daughters
                                                          of flesh,
gods and goddesses of flesh and blood.
We ask for bread and they give us hunger,
we ask for respect and they try to bribe us.
We will not kneel,
this is not the time to pray.
We will not wait for them to crucify our belief

para que resuciten nuevas democracias,
en nuestras manos la esperanza de levantar la vida
y honrar la sangre de los que hundieron
el anhelo como anzuelo a la tierra,
aferrados al consuelo de devolvernos la esperanza.
Los que custodiamos los sueños en las noches baldías
no instigaremos en el llanto de las madres que hacen patria
con los nombres de sus hijos muertos.

that we can breathe life into new democracies,
it is up to us to praise the life
and honor the blood of those who buried
their longing like a talisman in the earth,
clinging to the consolation that they gave us back our hope.
We who stand guard over dreams through empty nights
will not intrude on the weeping of mothers who build the
                                                                country
with the names of their dead sons and daughters.

**Bajo el tálamo**

*24-2-10 Victimarios de Yaneth Zepeda siguen libres semanas después de en¬contrado el cadáver de la mujer activista del Frente Nacional de la Resistencia Po¬pular de Honduras, Vanessa Yaneth Zepeda, las autoridades hondureñas no han encontrado a los responsables. Los empleados de la morgue no quieren hablar.*
*(Noticia de diario)*

Tu casa guarda un secreto,
una botija de oro se esconde bajo el tálamo,
sumergida en el barro
una serpiente agita el cuero,
muta una y otra vez,
sigilosa marca el camino de todo reptil atado a tu pie.
Será tiempo de sequía,
no madurarán las brozas de luz en tus silencios.
Será un viento subterráneo el que enderece tu espalda,
el que aniquile sin piedad los restos del desquicio.
¿Mueres de sed?
Lluévete dentro,
dentro de las piedras que besas en el río,
dentro del sol que enrojece tus hombros,
dentro de la serpiente que vistes
para mutar desde el dolor.

## Under the Marriage Bed

*2/24/10 Assassins of the victim remain at large. Weeks after the discovery of the body of Vanessa Yaneth Zepeda, activist with the Honduran National Front of Popular Resistance, Honduran authorities have not found the perpetrators of the crime. Workers at the morgue have declined to comment.*
*(Newspaper item)*

Your house holds a secret,
golden treasure hidden under the marriage bed,
deep in the mud
a snake slithers from its skin,
shedding again and again,
it watches, traces the path of every reptile tied to your foot.
It must be the dry season,
the dead leaves of light will not awaken in your silences.
It must be a subterranean wind that stiffens your back,
that pitilessly wipes out confusion's debris.
Are you dying of thirst?
Rain inside yourself,
inside the stones you kiss from the river,
inside the sun that reddens your shoulders,
inside the snake you wear
to shed your pain.


*[Translations by Janet N. Gold]*

## STELLA ("TITA") PINEDA BECERRA
## (Tegucigalpa, 1923)

**FILOSOFANDO**

¡Qué horrible es la vejez!
Se pierde el brillo de los ojos.
Se pierde parte de la memoria.
Se pierde la tersura de la piel.
Se pierde la verticalidad de la columna.
Se pierde la elegancia en el andar.
Se pierde la elasticidad de los músculos.
Se pierden los dientes.
Se pierde la erección.
Se pierde el color del cabello.
Se pierde el apetito sexual.
Se pierde la vista.
Se pierde el oído.
Se pierde en muchas cosas el deseo de vivir... pero...
¡Qué maravilloso es estar vivo!
Algunos pesimistas se preguntarán, entonces. ¿Qué nos queda?

Disfrutar el hecho de estar vivos.
Disfrutar los recuerdos de lo bello que fue la niñez,

## STELLA ("TITA") PINEDA BECERRA

From childhood she developed a solid social and revolutionary consciousness, totally generous; "Communist" they called her, like they did anyone who sought to build a society with better living conditions for all women and men. She and her late husband, Lorenzo Zelaya Alger, another revolutionary, had three daughters and two sons–Vickie, Sandra, Lorena, Héctor and Fernando. At age ninety, she still fights and is in the resistance. She has written numerous articles that were published in newspapers until the editors began to reject them due to their sharp, strong protest against injustice and inequality. An indefatigable writer and reader, full of positive energy that she transfers to all who know or meet her. Published book: *Consejos de una nonagenaria* (Advice from a Nonagenarian, 2013).


## PHILOSOPHIZING

Old age is horrible!
You lose the brightness in your eyes.
You lose part of your memory.
You lose the tautness of your skin.
You lose the straightness of your spine.
You lose elegance in your walk.
You lose elasticity in your muscles.
You lose your teeth.
You lose your erection.
You lose the color of your hair.
You lose your appetite for sex.
You lose your sight.
You lose your hearing.
You lose in many senses the desire to live... but...
It's so marvelous to be alive!
Some pessimists will ask, then, what is left for us to do?

Enjoy the fact of being alive.
Enjoy the memories of how beautiful childhood,

la juventud y la madurez.
Disfrutar del amor y del cariño que tuvimos con nuestro compañero.
Disfrutar de nuestros hijos e hijas.
Disfrutar de nuestros nietos y nietas.
Disfrutar de nuestros bisnietos y bisnietas.
Disfrutar de la naturaleza, del sol, de la luna, las estrellas, el mar el bosque, la música, de la belleza de esos árboles enormes copados de flores de vivos colores.
Disfrutar de una buena comida.
Disfrutar de nuestras amistades.
Disfrutar el poder compartir nuestras experiencias, nuestras vivencias y de nuestras pertenencias.
Disfrutar el poder seguir en lucha y resistencias.

Disfrutar, a lo máximo, de lo que nos queda de vida, pensando siempre en la suerte que hemos tenido de llegar
    a la vejez, viviendo lo que aún nos queda de existencia
        con la mayor intensidad.

youth and adulthood were.
Enjoy the love and closeness we had with our partner.
Enjoy our sons and daughters.
Enjoy our grandsons and granddaughters.
Enjoy our great grandsons and great granddaughters.
Enjoy nature, the sun, the moon, the stars, the sea
the forest, music, the beauty of tall trees
crowned in richly colored flowers.
Enjoy a good meal.
Enjoy our friends.
Enjoy the ability to share our experiences,
our learnings, our belongings.
Enjoy the ability to continue in struggle and resistances.

Enjoy to the utmost what is left of our life,
always remembering the luck we have had to arrive
      at old age, living what is left of our existence
      with the greatest intensity.

## LIBERTAD

¡Quiero ser libre como el mar!
libre, como el ave que vuela
sin cesar, bajo el límpido cielo.

Libre como el sol, la brisa o
la liebre que cruza fugaz
por la blanca y serpenteada carretera

Libre como los pájaros,
como las fieras, libre.
Libre como el viento
que viaja a las lejanías
sin decir a dónde va.

Libre como los niños
que, con imaginación,
llegan hasta Shangrilá.

Libre como el agua cristalina
que desciende de la montaña
y que va sembrando vida por doquier.

No quiero detenerme,
ni quiero descansar
quiero ser libre siempre
para poder volar!

**FREEDOM**

I want to be free like the sea!
free, like the bird that flies
endlessly, in the pristine sky.

Free like the sun, the breeze, or
the hare that quickly rushes
across the white, snaking highway

Free as the birds,
as the animals, free.
Free as the wind
that travels to far off places
not saying where it is going.

Free as children
who, with their imagination,
even reach Shangri-La.

Free as crystal clear water
that flows down the mountain
and sows life all about.

I don't want to stop,
I don't want to rest,
I want to be free always
so that I can fly!

*[Translations by María Roof]*

## AMADA ESPERANZA PONCE
(Tegucigalpa, 1983)

**Introspección**

Suena el silbato, rechinan los dientes
columnas de humo se balancean sobre sus fauces
antimotines, antimontones, antiverdad, antiguo antifaz.

Cae uno sobre otro
y vuelven sobre los alaridos del tiempo
de quién es la culpa
la culpa no basta.

Es hora de gritar
romper a gritos los oídos sordos.

Es hora de llevar a cuestas canciones
y cantar a la ignorancia de lo no dicho.

Es hora de correr contraídos por el viento
si se acercan estamos listos
alerta, alerta, ALERTA!

## AMADA ESPERANZA PONCE

Journalist, researcher, and writer. Director of the digital newspaper *Conexihon.info* of the Committee for Free Expression (C-Libre). Former editor of the digital version of the newspaper *La Tribuna*. Secretary of the National Association of Honduran Women Writers (ANDEH); cofounder of the "Máscara Suelta" Literary Cultural Collective; member of the Hispanoworld Union of Writers (UHE), the International Network of Editors and Alternative Projects (RIEPA), and the Central American Network of Cultural Journalists. Works published in various magazines and newspaper of Central America.

### Introspection

The whistle blows, teeth gnash
columns of smoke rise swirling above their maws
riot squads, crowd control, anti-truth, ancient mask.

One falls upon the other
and they return astride the shrieks of time
who is to blame
blame is not enough.

Now is the time to cry out
shout out to burst through deaf eardrums.

Now is the time to hoist our songs
and sing to the ignorance of the unspoken.

Now is the time to rush contracted by the wind
if they approach we are ready
Be ready, be ready, BE READY!

**Resonaban como profecías...**

Solo recordé las historias de tiempos que creía perdidos,
las voces de mi madre resonaron en mis oídos
de aquellos momentos... de la década de los 80's
de aquellos que nunca, jamás, se deben dejar en el olvido.

Recordé que no quería callarse nunca
y de cómo se perdieron las vidas de sus amigos.
Mira como son las cosas, madre, pareciera que todo regresa/
    -le dije.
Pero ella respondió: nunca, nunca se han ido.

**They Resounded like Prophecies . . .**

I only remembered the stories of times I believed to be behind us,
the words of my mother resounded in my ears
of those times... of the decade of the 80's
of those who never, ever, should pass into oblivion.

I remembered how she never wanted not to speak out
and how the lives of her friends were lost.
Look how things are now, mother, it would seem everything
                              comes back again/-I told her.
But she replied: never, ever did it go away.

**La cárcel**

Convertida en sombra
al oriente de esta Honduras
los ayeres de una democracia fingida retornan.

Pero su cuerpo resiste
bajo la luz de El Paraíso.

Las voces calladas de los medios
gritan en las paredes de la catedral
¿Quién apaciguó los llantos de los mugrosos?

**Jail**

Converted to shadow
in the east of this Honduras
the yesterdays of a pretend democracy return.

But its body resists
beneath the light of El Paraíso.

The voices muffled in the media
shout out on the walls of the cathedral
Who calmed the cries of the unwashed?

*[Translations by Gail Ament]*

# RACHEL RAMÍREZ
(Agua Blanca Sur, El Progreso, Yoro, 1956)

## LAS LOCURAS DE MEL

Los ricos le llaman loco a nuestro presidente constitucional, José Manuel Zelaya Rosales. Nosotros creemos que si su pensamiento ha tenido rasgos de locura, se trata de una locura productiva, una locura altruista, una locura de amor al pueblo.

Los ricos dicen que Mel está loco. Lo dicen porque, siendo un propietario de considerable fortuna, lo normal hubiera sido que se pusiera de parte de los millonarios, pero se puso de parte de los pobres. Desde la lógica de los ricos, un rico tiene que estar loco cuando se le ocurre soñar con que todos los hondureños y hondureñas tenemos derecho, al menos, a las condiciones indispensables de sobrevivencia. Loco el hombre. Porque siendo presidente, estando en las mieles del poder, se negó a ser uno más de la serie de figurones insensibles que han pasado por la silla presidencial y, contrario a lo que sus amigos esperaban de él, José Manuel Zelaya echó su suerte a favor de la gente humilde.

Fue así como decidió que no pagaran electricidad las familias cuyos bienes materiales no pasaran de un ventilador, un televisor, una pequeña refrigeradora, unos cuantos bombillos fluorescentes y tal vez una plancha eléctrica (pues los pobres ya nos acostumbramos a llevar ajadas no sólo las vestimentas sino también las tristezas del alma):

## RACHEL RAMÍREZ

Writer, free thinker, feminist, member of the Women's Forum for Life, human rights defender, with training from the Committee of Relatives of Disappeared Detainees in Honduras (COFADEH). Degree in Biology and Chemistry, Francisco Morazán National Pedagogical University (UPNFM). Professor, retired in 2007 with pension of 5,000 lempiras (about $250) after fifteen years of service. "Thanks to another of Mel's acts of madness, the INPREMAH (National Institute for Teachers) had no other choice but to raise my pension to 5,500 lempiras" (about $275). Published poetry: *Sol de lo oscuro* (Sun from the Dark Side, 2003).

## MEL'S MADNESSES

The rich call our constitutionally elected president, José Manuel Zelaya Rosales, mad. We believe that if his thinking has shown signs of madness, then it's a productive madness, an altruistic madness, a madness of love for the people.

The rich say Mel is mad. They say that because, since he's a landowner of considerable wealth, the normal thing would have been for him to side with the millionaires, but he sided with the poor. In the logic of the rich, a rich man must be mad when he dreams that all of us Honduran men and women have the right, at the very least, to the basic conditions for survival. The man is mad. Because as president, enjoying the sweetness of power, he refused to be just another in a long line of insensitive characters who have passed through the presidential office. Contrary to what his friends expected of him, José Manuel Zelaya cast his lot with humble folk.

And so it was that he decided to suspend electric bills for families whose material wealth didn't go beyond a fan, a TV set, a small refrigerator, a few fluorescent light bulbs, and maybe an electric iron (we the poor are used to wearing not only tatty clothes on our bodies but also well-worn heartaches in our souls):

el presidente sabía que los pobres aguantamos hambre, que nuestros bienes materiales generalmente son de cuarta, de quinta o hasta de octava mano; él sabía que colocamos remiendo sobre remiendo, que cada día es una angustia por no saber qué vamos a darles de comer a nuestros hijos. Siendo él un miembro de la aristocracia, se decidió por los pobres. "¡Tiene que estar loco!", bramaron los magnates.

Del pensamiento pasó a los hechos: Mientras él fue presidente, más de 600,000 (dije seiscientas mil) familias tuvimos electricidad gratis, quiero decir que jamás pagamos ni un centavo a ENEE; incluso hubo una época en que no sólo no nos cobraban sino que al ir al banco el cajero, a nombre del Gobierno, nos daba entre cien y ciento cincuenta lempiras, como ayuda solidaria. Nosotros no pagábamos electricidad porque el Gobierno de Mel Zelaya nos la regalaba; pero los magnates no pagan electricidad porque se la roban, y no hay poder en el mundo que los meta a la cárcel. Sus fábricas y sus empresas consumen la electricidad que paga la clase media hondureña.

Mel, como toda la gente de buena voluntad, tiene loco el corazón. Es un loco soñador. Soñaba y ponía en práctica sus sueños. Un buen día los padres de familia de Honduras fueron exonerados del pago de matrícula en los centros educativos oficiales; y en cierto momento los niños y las niñas comenzaron a recibir merienda en su escuela; y de un día para otro declaró la guerra al analfabetismo; y otro día aumentó el número de médicos para que cuidaran completamente gratis de la salud del pueblo; y otro día hizo una ley para brindarle seguro social a las empleadas domésticas; y los campesinos recibieron títulos de sus parcelas y semilla mejorada y préstamos para las siembras y la opción a usar los tractores de los que regaló Venezuela al pueblo hondureño (pero la burocracia al servicio de los ricos enredó las cosas y los tractores nunca fueron entregados a los campesinos).

Los pobres sí compartimos los sueños locos de Mel; cómo no abrazar el sueño de que todas las familias que viven abajo de la línea de la pobreza recibieran un bono de casi tres mil lempiras. Seguramente muchas de las familias que recibieron el bono solidario nunca habían tenido de junto esa suma de dinero.

the president knew that we poor people bear hunger, that our material possessions are generally third hand or fifth or even eighth hand. He knew that we patch our patches, that every day we anguish over what we're going to feed our children. Being a member of the aristocracy, he opted for the poor. "Surely he's mad!" bellowed the fat cats.

He went from thought to action: while he was president, more than 600,000 (I said six hundred thousand) families got free electricity; I mean we never paid even a cent to the ENEE [National Electric Energy Agency]. There was even a time when they not only didn't charge us, they gave us humanitarian assistance of one hundred to one hundred fifty lempiras in the name of the Government when we went to the teller at the bank. We didn't pay for electricity because the Government of Mel Zelaya gave it to us for free. But the fat cats don't pay for electricity because they steal it, and there's no power in the world that can put them in jail. Their factories and businesses consume electricity that the Honduran middle class pays for.

Mel, like all people of good will, is crazy at heart. He's a crazy dreamer. He would dream and then put his dreams into practice. One fine day Honduran parents were exonerated from paying for the registration of their children at public schools. And then children began receiving a free lunch at school; from one day to the next he declared war on illiteracy; and then he raised the number of doctors who would offer free healthcare to the public; and then he made a law to give social security to domestic workers; and farmers received titles to their plots of land and improved seed and loans for their plantings and the option to use tractors that Venezuela gave to the Honduran people (but the bureaucracy beholden to the rich tied things up, so the tractors were never delivered to the farmers).

Yes, we poor people share Mel's mad dreams. Who wouldn't embrace the dream that all families that live below the poverty line might receive a bonus of practically three thousand lempiras [about $150]? Certainly, many of the families who received the solidarity bonus had never seen that much money at once before.

Es verdad que muchos de los sueños de Mel se perdieron como por arte de magia entre las manos de algunos de sus "colaboradores", pero también es verdad cientos de miles de desposeídos vieron el sueño de Mel hecho realidad. Y mientras los pobres gozaban el sueño de Mel, el insomnio asaltó a los magnates, a esos magnates, a ésos en cuyos zapatos Florsheim aún rechinan las arenas de los desiertos del Medio Oriente, de donde llegaron hace poco más de medio siglo, con una mano adelante y la otra atrás; esos magnates que se han apoderado de la política hondureña, de las cúpulas religiosas, del fútbol, de los medios masivos de comunicación, de los negocios libres de impuestos. Esos son los que no volvieron a pegar un ojo, ante la realidad de los sueños locos de Mel. Otros que dejaron de dormir tranquilos fueron algunos revolucionarios que se hacen llamar marxistas y que (¡qué risa!) no aceptaban a Mel porque "Mel no es marxista".

Está bien que los magnates y algunos mal llamados marxistas no quieran a Mel. Pero habemos millones que lo queremos. ¿Quiénes somos los que queremos a Mel? Somos la gente que vive en las aldeas, en los campos bananeros, los que hemos aguantado hambre siempre, los intelectuales de alta sensibilidad humana, los revolucionarios sin etiquetas estúpidas, la gente pobre de las ciudades, la clase media consciente, quienes que no tenemos más currículum que las manos encallecidas, en fin, el pueblo. Lo queremos porque en él vemos la esencia de nuestra tierra. Los magnates dirán que Mel ayudó a la gente sencilla para llegarles al corazón. Muy bien, que lo digan. Lo cierto es que quien nos regala un pescado y quiere enseñarnos a pescar merece que lo quieran. ¡Qué bueno, Mel Zelaya optó por ganarse el corazón de nosotros mediante el método de devolvernos la dignidad! La pregunta fundamental es: ¿Por qué ustedes, magnates, nunca hicieron nada parecido? Queremos a Mel porque es el primer presidente que se interesó por la suerte de los que nada tenemos; ustedes sólo pensaron en nosotros para ver el mejor modo de arrancarnos la alegría y nuestra fuerza de trabajo. Vistas así las cosas, tienen ustedes razón de llamar loco a Mel.

It's true that many of Mel's dreams got lost, as if by magic, in the hands of some of his "collaborators," but it's also true that hundreds of thousands of the dispossessed saw Mel's dream come true. And while the poor enjoyed Mel's dream, insomnia beset the fat cats, those tycoons whose Florsheim shoes still squeaked with sand from Middle Eastern deserts, where they had come from just a half century earlier, with nothing but one hand out front and the other in back; those tycoons who had taken control of Honduran politics, of religious leadership, of soccer, of mass media, of tax-free businesses. Those are the ones who could never close an eye, facing the reality of Mel's mad dreams. Others who no longer slept soundly were the revolutionaries who call themselves Marxists and who (how laughable!) didn't accept Mel because "Mel's not a Marxist."

It's fine if the fat cats and some so-called Marxists don't like Mel. But there are millions of us who love him. Who are we? We're the folks who live in the villages, in the banana fields, those who've always endured hunger, intellectuals of high human sensitivities, revolutionaries without stupid labels, the urban poor, a sensible and informed middle class—we have no professional portfolio other than our calloused hands. In short, we're the people. We love him because in him we see the essence of our land. The fat cats will say that Mel helped the simple folks in order to win their hearts. Fine, let them say that. What's certain is that he who gives us a fish and also wants to teach us to fish deserves our love. How great that Mel chose to win our hearts by giving us back our dignity! The fundamental question is this: Why, fat cats, did you never do anything like that? We love Mel because he's the first president who cared about those of us who have nothing. You have thought of us only to find the best way to snatch away our happiness and usurp our labor. Seeing things this way, you have good reason to call Mel mad.

En su locura, Mel se negó a entrar en negocios con las "Sagradas Familias" de este país; eso no se lo perdonaron, pues si hubiera hecho negocios con ellos, podrían haberlo manipulado, podrían "amablemente" haberle torcido el brazo en las conversaciones de sobremesa. Eso no lo pudieron hacer, ¡qué rabia! Pero la cresta más alta de la ola de su locura llegó cuando propuso que los chuñas, los chucos, los analfabetas funcionales o no funcionales debíamos tener derecho a construir una nueva patria a través de la redacción de una nueva Constitución. Fue esto lo que rompió los siete cielos que cubren este país: Los cancerberos, los dueños de la patria por decreto divino, sacaron a los gendarmes del Apocalipsis, y, en contubernio con los Halcones más Poderosos de la Tierra, derrumbaron la casa de las y los verdaderos hondureños.

¡Qué loco que está Mel! Y su locura es tan contagiosa que los propietarios comerciales de este país ya no saben qué hacer con tantas y tantos locos dispuestos a ofrendar la vida por la patria que sueña Mel y por defendernos a como dé lugar.

*28 de julio 2009*

In his madness, Mel refused to enter into negotiations with the "Holy Families" of this country. This they never forgave him: if he had dealt with them, they could have manipulated him, they could have "nicely" twisted his arm in after-dinner conversations. But this they couldn't do. They were furious! Like a wave, his madness reached its highest crest when he proposed that we, the barefoot and filthy, the functionally and not so functionally illiterate, should have the right to build a new country through the drafting of a new Constitution. This was what broke the seven heavens that cover this country: the Cerberuses—the gatetenders, the divinely decreed owners of this country, called forth the gendarmes of the Apocalypse, and in conspiracy with the Most Powerful Falcons of the Earth, they brought down the house of the true Hondurans.

How mad is Mel! And his madness is so contagious that the business owners of this country no longer know what to do with so many crazy women and men ready to give our lives for the country Mel dreams of and to defend ourselves, by any means necessary.

*July 28, 2009*

[Translation by Linda J. Craft]

# DÉBORAH RAMOS
(Río Lindo, Cortés, 1962)

**El canto de Mel y su pueblo en resistencia**
canto III
De los santos pérfidos y otros males

Entre los dueños de las escaleras que llevan al cielo, vi viles carroñeros que prostituían la palabra bendita, se autodenominaban santos, apóstoles y profetas y vi la baba de la ignominia correr por todo lo ancho y largo de sus sacros templos, templos construidos para asaltar la fe en su tristísima ignorancia; y así, se nacieron los santos inventores, videntes del porvenir, conocedores de pasados, presentes y futuros, descubridores de lunas cuadradas, de hacedores de oasis en el más grande desierto de la palabra hambre.
Luego fabricaron un espejismo profético de fantasmas y molinos de viento que hacían muecas desde una isla, gigantes sancochadores de niños, roba aliento de muchachos púberos, encantadores del cono sur, con aliento a petróleo y crearon la santa inquisición y excomulgaron niños en cárceles, convirtiendo Al Paraíso en campo de concentración donde expiaban las culpas niños, niñas, jóvenes, mujeres, hombres, que pensaban en la libertad y pensaron en desollarles la esperanza porque el pensamiento nuevo huele a comunismo y al no poder secuestrar a Dios crearon un Dios nuevo, lo vistieron con uniforme militar y lo llenaron de barras y estrellas y esto lo hicieron en el antes y en el después de la historia.

# DÉBORAH RAMOS

Poet, educator, cultural promoter and children's storyteller. University degree in Letters from the National Autonomous University (UNAH). Poems published in anthologies, journals, and national and international newspapers.

## Mel's Song and His People in Resistance
Canto III
Of Perfidious Saints and Other Evils

Among the owners of the stairways leading to heaven, I saw vile carrion-feasters who prostituted the holy word, named themselves saints, apostles and prophets, and I saw the drooling of ignominy flow the entire length and breadth of their sacred temples, temples built to assault the faith in its saddest ignorance; and that is how saint inventors were born, prescient about the future, knowers of pasts, presents, and futures, discoverers of squared moons, of the makers of oases in the greatest desert of the word hunger.
Then, they created a prophetic mirage of phantoms and windmills that made faces from an island, gigantic stewers of children, breath-thieves of pubescent youth, enchanters from the southern cone, with oily breath, and they created the holy inquisition and excommunicated children in jails, turning El Paraíso into a concentration camp where boys, girls, young people, women, men expiated their sins—that they thought of freedom, and they planned to skin their hope alive, because new thought reeks of communism, and since they couldn't kidnap God they created a new God, dressed him in a military uniform and filled him with stars and stripes and this they did in the before and after of historical story.

Y los santos inquisidores fabricantes de la mentira siguieron proyectando en pantallas gigantes a los Espartacos de América y desde sus púlpitos los señalaban ¡Esos son los falsos profetas! ¡Los que te harán compartir lo que tienes! ¡Los que harán que tú seas igual al otro! Los que harán que el Cristo de la vida multiplique los panes para todos. Y tuvieron miedo, mucho miedo, tanto miedo que todo el que levantaba su puño era llamado a ser exorcizado por el golpe del tolete, el gas mortal o la bala asesina, eran encarcelados y llevados a la hoguera de la tortura.

Y fue así como aparecieron los santos pérfidos excomulgadores de las palabras que vuelan, de los pasos en marchas, de los puños en alto, de los gritos de protesta y vi los fusiles hacer misas y vi las bombas lacrimógenas predicar un extraño evangelio de podredumbre frente a púlpitos de vergüenza y el verdadero Dios, desde su lugar, en todas partes, se tapó la cara con sus manos de amor y el Cristo obrero cargaba en sus hombros a cada hombre cansado, perseguido, excomulgado. Resucitaba a los mártires como Lázaro y les decía Levántate y camina que la patria los necesita y fue así que nadie moría porque aún la muerte se resistía a ver caer al pueblo.

And the holy inquisitors creators of the lie continued projecting onto gigantic screens the Spartacuses of America and from their pulpits pointed at them: Those are the false prophets! They will make you share what you have! They will make you the same as everyone else! They will make the living Christ multiply the breads for everyone. And they were afraid, very afraid, so afraid that each one who raised his fist was called to be exorcised by the blow of a club, lethal gas or murderous bullet, jailed and carried off to the bonfire of torture.

And thus it was that the perfidious saints appeared, excommunicators of words that soar, of steps in marches, of fists held high, of screams of protest and I saw rifles say church masses and I saw teargas bombs preach a strange gospel of putrescence from pulpits of shame, and the true God, from his place, everywhere, covered his face with his hands of love and Christ the worker hoisted onto his shoulders every man who was tired, persecuted, excommunicated. He resuscitated martyrs like Lazarus and said to them: "Rise up and walk, for the nation needs you," and that was how no one died because death resisted seeing the people fall.

**El amor en los tiempos del golpe**

El amor es resistente en resistencia, mi amor. Tú marchando, amando con tu puño en alto, sosteniendo en tu boca la palabra colectiva, sangrando tu brazo en el abrazo, que es mi brazo con que abrazamos a todos los hermanos y hermanas. Queriéndonos en multitud, enjugándonos las lágrimas que surgen del dolor de masas. Somos románticos; nos amamos con esa pasión proletaria, con esa ternura infinita que duele cuando se hace bajo la lluvia de bombas lacrimógenas, de golpes de toletes, de gases mortales. Te amo tanto porque me amas y te amo y los dos amamos la patria.

¡Qué amor, mi hermano! Hoy que te siento más mi hermano, hoy que haces caminos con tus pasos, hoy que no guardas silencio y que tu palabra es fusil en guardia, hoy que tus manos heridas sangran por mis manos, hoy que me alegro de verte y decirte que sería feliz muriendo por ti en esta batalla. ¡Ay, mi hermano! Nunca fui tan feliz de verte cargando la misma cruz en este calvario.

¡Cuánto amor desbocado en esas calles! Caminantes aguerridos, como enamorados, agarrados de las manos, sintiendo la rebeldía que se siente cuando se ama. ¡Ay, amor! Cuánto tenemos en común, tú pensando como yo y yo pensando como tú y los dos pensando como todos los que marchan con la patria.

Mi amigo, nunca habíamos sido tan uno. Mira cómo cargamos juntos la esperanza y en esta noche oscura en que las fieras han salido de sus madrigueras, tú estás aquí, yo estoy aquí, todos estamos aquí con las manos tuyas, las mías y las de todos empuñando la antorcha que nos lleve a un mañana.

Ay, mi hermano, cuánto amor hay en esta lucha, aquí, compartiendo el pan multiplicado, bebiéndonos este cáliz colectivo, reviviendo con nuestro aliento la herencia de nuestros ancestros, creando un patrimonio de dignidad para nuestros hijos.

Ay, mi amado, tú con el puño en alto, yo con el fusil de mi pluma en la mano. Tú golpeando con tu

## Love in the Times of the Coup

Love is resistant in resistance, my love. You marching, loving with your fist held high, protecting in your mouth the collective word, your arm bleeding in the embrace, which is my arm with which we embrace all our brothers and sisters. Loving each other in the multitude, wiping our tears that rise from the pain of masses. We are romantics; we love each other with that proletarian passion, with that infinite tenderness that aches when it happens under the rain of teargas bombs, of police-club blows, of lethal gases. I love you so much because you love me and I love you and we both love our country.

What a love, my brother! Today I feel that you are even more my brother, today as you create paths as you walk, today when you are not silent and your word is a rifle at the ready, today when your wounded hands bleed for my hands, today when I am happy to see you and tell you I would be happy dying for you in this battle. Oh, my brother! I was never so happy to see you carrying the same cross in this calvary.

So much love unleashed in those streets! Valiant marchers, like lovers, holding hands, feeling the rebellion you feel when you love. Oh, love! We have so much in common, you thinking like me and I thinking like you and both of us thinking like all those who are marching with our nation.

My friend, never had we been so much like one. Look how together we carry hope and in this dark night in which the beasts have left their lairs, you are here, I am here, we are all here with your hands, mine, and those of everyone hoisting the torch that will take us to a tomorrow.

Oh, my brother, so much love is in this struggle, here, sharing the bread multiplied, drinking from this collective chalice, reviving with our breath the legacy of our ancestors, creating a patrimony of dignity for our children.

Oh, my beloved, you with your fist held high, I with the rifle of my pen in my hand. You hammering with your

grito, yo disparando con la palabra; tú caminante guerrero, yo en esta trinchera de ideas; tú levantando al hermano, yo nutriendo la batalla con este sentimiento hecho poema. ¡Ay, mi amado, qué grande amor es éste, que acunamos a la patria en nuestros brazos! Ay, mi amado; ay, mi amigo; ay, mi hermano... Cuánto amor desgajado en esas calles: mi hermano Obed, mi hermana Wendy, mi hermano Roger y todos los demás hermanos... Mira, nos sonríen, traen ramitos de olivo entre sus labios.

shout, I firing with the word; you marching warrior, I in this entrenchment of ideas; you raising your brother, I nourishing the battle with this sentiment made into a poem. Oh, my beloved, what a great love this is, as we are nestling the country in our arms! Oh, my beloved; oh, my friend; oh, my brother... So much love wrenched away on those streets: my brother Obed, my sister Wendy, my brother Roger, and all the other brothers and sisters... Look, they smile at us, they bring olive branches between their lips.

**El canto de los dioses malos**

El día que le quebraron
los geranios a mi patria
los casi veinte dioses malos de Xibalbá
elevaron una pirámide
del tamaño de la mentira
se vistieron con piel de cordero
elevaron pañuelos blancos
como si fueran de acá
y escondieron sus turbantes de corsarios
y así entonaron un nuevo canto
un canto que no es el nuestro

## The Song of the Bad Gods

The day they broke off
the geraniums in my country
the almost twenty bad gods of Xibalbá
built a pyramid
the size of the lie
dressed up in lambskin
raised white handkerchiefs
as if they were from here
and hid their pirate turbans
and began to sing a new song
a song that is not our song


*[Translations by María Roof]*

# FRANCESCA RANDAZZO
(Tegucigalpa, 1973)

**Soy ese ruido**

"Soy ese ruido, ese ruido de las olas.
Y fuera de eso,
Poco más.
Una colección de palabras
A las que a veces doy un sentido.
Una colección
Pequeña de palabras."

# FRANCESCA RANDAZZO

Poet, editor, translator (Spanish, English, French, Italian). Winner of Robert Sosa Young Poetry Prize, 1997. Doctorate in Sociology, University of Santiago de Compostela (USC), Spain, 2012; Diploma in Advanced Studies, USC, 2010; Master in Social Sciences, FLACSO, Guatemala, 2005; degree in Languages, National Autonomous University (UNAH); degree in Languages and Mathematics, France, 1992. Assistant director, *Revista Sociología y Tecnociencia* (Sociology and Technoscience Journal), Málaga, Spain; editor and head of publications, *YAXKIN* journal, Honduras. Collaborator in the Street Children and Youth Project, and Physicians without Borders. Teacher at the French-Honduran High School, 1996-2003. Books published: *Honduras, patria de la espera* (Honduras, Country of Waiting, 2011); *Nuevas posibilidades de los imaginarios sociales* (New Possibilities for Social Imaginaries, 2011); *Barcos en el aire* (Ships in the Air, 2008); *Compás de luz* (Compass of Light, 2003); *A mar abierto* (On the Open Sea, 2000); *Roce de tierra* (Touch of Earth, 1998).

## I Am That Noise

"I am that noise, that noise of waves.
And besides that,
Little more.
A collection of words
To which I sometimes give a meaning.
A small collection
Of words."

## Dónde está el calor

Dónde está el calor
Ese ambiente ligero
      Desenfadado
En el que navegabas poeta
Dónde quedó
Sin contratiempos entre el caos
Tu horizonte radiante y azul
Ahora el frío
Descubre los perros, los postes
Los muertos
Los guardias congelados
Cuidando la casa del amo
El hielo
De sus armas
En acecho
Una masa de policías
Levita y fermenta en la noche
Sin color sin palomas
Sin árboles
Sin casas sin esquinas sin callejones
Sólo añicos sólo golpes
Y un reloj
Que marca
El toque de queda

## Where Is the Warmth

Where is the warmth
That light ambiance
      Relaxed
In which you sailed poet
Where did it stay
Your radiant blue horizon
Without obstacles among the chaos
Now the cold
Discovers dogs, posts
The dead
The freezing sentinels
Guarding over the house of the master
The ice
Of their weapons
Lying in wait
A dough of policemen
Rises and ferments in the night
Without color without doves
Without trees
Without houses without corners without alleys
Only shattered pieces only blows
And a clock
That marks
The hour of curfew.

## Tierra que se mueve

Perezosa
     Tibia
     Húmeda
Fuego que late
     En la lejanía de los tiempos
Tierra compacta que es
Nuevamente
     Espacio de siembra
     Lugar de semilla
Imagen que centella
     Inquieta
     Al borde de la Salvación
Como un soplo
Enceguecedor
     El tiempo de
     Los dominadores
Relampaguea con su látigo
     Hemos sido esperados
     Hoy
     Día del Juicio Final
Código genético
     De un tiempo mesiánico
Gruta llanura
Símbolo que llamarás
Para llenar la ausencia
Presente susurrando
Aún
No
Me
Has
Perdido
Barro
Savia animal
De la historia
     Cita permanente
Reclamada en su crónica

## Land that Moves

Lazy
    Tepid
    Humid
Fire that beats
    In the distance of times
Compact land that is
Again
    Space for sowing
    Place for seed
Image that sparkles
    Uneasy
    On the edge of Salvation
Like a blinding
Breeze
    The time of
    The dominators
Flashes with its whip
    We have been awaited
    Today
    Judgment Day
Genetic code
    Of a messianic time
Grotto plain
Symbol that you will call
To fill the present
Absence whispering
You
Have
Not yet
Lost
Me
Clay
Animal lifeblood
Of history
    Permanent date
Claimed in its chronicle

Curso marino
    Golfo bahía
Corriente que rescatarás de la sombra
    Y subirá por tu cuerpo
    Y será entre nosotros
    Signo de miradas
    Lenguaje familiar
    Resistencia

Marine course
> Gulf bay
Current that you will rescue from shadow
> And it will rise through your body
> And it will be among us
> Sign of glances
> Familiar language
> Resistance

*[Translations by María Roof]*

# MARÍA LUISA REGALADO MORÁN
**(Ocotepeque, 1959)**

**A mi niña**

A mi niña
de cabellera negra,
lisa y muy larga,
de piel trigueña
curtida por el viento
por el frío
por la lluvia
por el lodo
por el sol
y  por el trabajo
desde muy temprana edad.

# MARÍA LUISA REGALADO MORÁN

Worked as a child and teenager alongside her mother and father, five sisters and two brothers at a hacienda. At age 14 she began participating in the Catholic church led by Father Fausto Milla and became a catechist and delegate of the Word of God. In the early 1980s she participated in the Honduran Federation of Rural Women (FEHMUC) and later was one of the founders of the Council for the Integral Development of the Rural Woman (CODIMCA). In 1989, she, Zoila Madrid, Lety Elvir and Ana Elsy Mendoza founded the League of Patriotic Women of Honduras (LIMUPH), now known as the Honduran Womens Collective (CODEMUH). She is General Coordinator of CODEMUH and represents the collective on the Tribunal of Women against Femicides (Tribuna de Mujeres contra los Femicidios) and the Central American Network of Organizations of Women in Solidarity with Maquila Workers (REDCAM). Most of her knowledge and skills were learned in the university of life. At the end of 1970 and in 1982 she learned to read and write through radio schooling and completed her elementary school studies with the Teacher in the Home program, designed by the Manuel Pagan Lozano Institute for programs in Distance Education. She has written the poems "Soy mujer rebelde" (I Am A Woman Rebel), "A mi niña" (To My Girl), and "Era de noche" (It Was at Night).

## To My Girl

To my girl
with the black hair,
straight and very long,
brown skin
burnt by the wind
by the cold
by the rain
by the mud
by the sun
by hard work
since early childhood.

A mi niña
flaca por su contextura,
y por la desnutrición.

A mi niña que sobrevivió
gracias a los vegetales
a los ayotes
a sus flores
y guías tiernas.
Gracias a los güisquiles
y a sus guías.
Gracias a la flor de izote
y a sus piños;
y a las guayabas.
Gracias a los aguacates,
 a los quiletes,
a los guates,
y a las yerbasmoras.
Gracias a los sabrosos subtes,
a los cangrejos de la quebrada
(y del pozo o de los matorrales de la milpa).
Gracias a los guineos,
mínimos, majonchos, criollos,
a los gracianos
y hasta los datilitos
(solo por mencionar algunos)
y también a los ricos tomatillos de gallina.

A mi niña
para quien el maíz y los frijoles
son un manjar,
desde muy pequeña aprendió
a cultivarlos.
Aprendió a tapiscar,
destusar y a desgranar el maíz.
Aprendió a cocer el nixtamal
y a quebrarlo en la piedra
(para hacer las ricas tortillas).
Aprendió a hacer el chilate
y la chigua de masa.

To my girl
thin by nature
and from malnutrition.

To my girl, who survived
thanks to vegetables,
squash
and its flowers
and tender shoots.
Thanks to the *güisquiles*
and their shoots.
Thanks to the flower of the *izote* palm
and its nuts,
and to guavas.
Thanks to avocados,
*quiletes,*
*guates*
and *yerbasmoras.*
Thanks to delicious *subtes,*
to crabs from the stream,
(and from the well and cornfield thickets).
Thanks to guineo plantains:
*mínimos, majonchos, criollos,*
and *gracianos,*
and even tiny dates
(just to mention a few)
and also the tasty *tomatillos de gallina.*

To my girl
for whom corn and beans
are a delicacy
she learned to grow
at an early age.
She learned to pick corn,
shuck the husks and shell kernels from the cob.
She learned to boil corn with lime to make *nixtamal*
and grind it on the stone
(to prepare delicious *tortillas*).
She learned to make *chilate*
and *chigua de masa.*

Aprendió a hacer las empanadas
de quiletes,
de ayote tierno y de sus flores.
Aprendió a raspar los elotes
para hacer los tamalitos,
las riguas,
atol dulce
y el atol chuco
(para tomarlo
acompañado de los elotes
sancochados o asados a la brasa).

A mi niña
maltratada por los adultos
y las adultas.
Por su padre y madre.
Maltratada por su hermano
y sus hermanas mayores.
Maltratada por el abuelo
y por particulares.

A mi niña de piel y cabellera hermosa:
curtida por el dolor,
por la angustia,
por la tristeza,
por la impotencia,
por el trabajo,
y por la confusión
(entre el amor,
el rencor,
la ternura,
la impotencia
y la ilusión).

Mi niña trabajaba
desde la madrugada
hasta muy, muy noche.
Trabajó desde muy pequeña
desde que su cerebro grabó los recuerdos.
Encerraba terneros,

She learned to make *empanadas*
of *quiletes*
and of tender squash and its flowers.
She learned to scrape corncobs
to make *tamalitos,*
*riguas,*
*atol dulce,*
and *atol chuco*
(to drink with ears of corn
steamed or grilled over coals).

To my girl
mistreated by adult men
and women.
By her father and mother.
Mistreated by her brother
and her older sisters.
Mistreated by her grandfather
and others not her kin.

To my girl with the beautiful skin and hair:
hardened by pain,
by sorrow,
by sadness,
by impotence,
by hard work,
and by confusion
(between love,
resentment,
tenderness
impotence
and hope).

My girl worked
from dawn
til very late at night.
She worked since she was little,
since memories were engraved in her brain.
She penned up calves,

arreaba y ordeñaba vacas,
sacaba mantequilla,
hacía cuajada,
queso
y hasta requesón (para el patrón).

Mi niña
de manos y pies rajados
por el contacto con el lodo,
con las espinas,
las piedras
y por los matorrales,
por tapiscar, destusar y desgranar maíz.
Por manipular los lazos
que amarraban a Sereno, el caballo (de su papá),
a la vaca,
y a los cerdos.

Mi niña
desde muy pequeña era rebelde
e ingeniosa.
Soñaba con salir de la hacienda
e irse lejos.
Terminar con la violencia
y la explotación
eran sus deseos.

Mi niña
sin saber qué era eso de "clase social"
desde su inocencia se conectaba con ella.
No entendía por qué su padre trabajaba
y les hacía trabajar (para otras personas)
sin recibir ingreso económico alguno
a pesar de tanta pobreza que vivían.

Mi niña
sin saber leer y escribir,
desde su adolescencia
dirigía los análisis de la Biblia;
cuestionaba las incoherencias

herded and milked cows,
churned butter,
made curds
and cheese
and even *requesón* (for the boss).

My girl
with hands and feet chapped
from contact with mud,
thorns,
rocks
and brambles,
from picking, shucking and shelling corn,
from handling ropes
to tie up Sereno, her father's horse,
the cow,
and the pigs.

My girl
since early childhood was defiant
and ingenious.
She dreamed of leaving the farm
and going far away.
Ending violence
and exploitation
was her wish.

My girl
without knowing the meaning of "social class,"
in her innocence connected to it.
She couldn't understand why her father worked
and made them work (for other people)
without any compensation
despite the extreme poverty in which they lived.

My girl
tho' not knowing how to read or write,
since adolescence
led Bible study,
questioning incoherencies

(que encontraba)
cuando su hermanita, la más chiquita,
o su compadre leían la biblia para ella.
Mi niña se preparaba
para dirigir los grupos eclesiales de base, la celebración
de la palabra de Dios,
y los grupos de oración.

Mi niña
sentía que existían cosas raras en la Biblia,
por ejemplo:
"era más fácil que un camello entrara por el ojo de una aguja
a que un rico entrara a los reinos del cielo",
(le parecía extraño)
como algo que motivaba
a que las personas se sintieran felices
de su empobrecimiento
porque de ellas
era el Reino de Dios.
Ella vivía en la miseria
y la pasaba muy mal.
Eso la confundía,
ella cuestionaba.

En su adolescencia
murió su madre, luego su padre,
mi niña
asumió como una madre
responsabilidades,
criando a dos hermanas
y a su hermano menor.
En sus espaldas cargó
con los nudos históricos
de la violencia
y la impotencia
por no haber podido decirles
del daño que le hicieron vivir.
Cargó con la responsabilidad materna
como una adulta.

(that she would find)
when her little sister, the youngest,
or her *compadre* read the Bible for her.
My girl prepared herself
to lead basic ecclesial groups, the celebration
of the word of God
and prayer circles.

My girl
felt there were strange things in the Bible,
for example:
"it's easier for a camel to pass through the eye of a needle,
than for a rich man to enter the kingdom of heaven,"
(it seemed odd to her)
like something that motivated
people to feel content
with their impoverishment
for theirs
was the Kingdom of God.
She lived in misery
and her life was hard.
She was confused,
she questioned.

During her adolescence,
her mother died, and then her father,
my girl
assumed motherly
responsibilities,
raising her two sisters
and her younger brother.
She shouldered
the historical weight
of violence
and impotence
for being unable to speak to them
of the damage they did to her.
She fulfilled her maternal obligations
like an adult.

Sintió el dolor por la pérdida
de su madre,
una mujer muy joven
con mucha fuerza,
Cincuenta y cinco años tenía.
Nunca pudo decirle
que (ella) la había violentado
con todas las pesadumbres
pero que la entendía
y la amaba.
Pronunciar la palabra "amor"
era vergonzoso
solo para ella,
su madre.

Mi niña
forzosamente se convirtió en adulta
y se enfrentó valientemente
a las prácticas de violencia
infligidas por su hermano mayor,
logrando liberarse ella,
y a sus hermanitas.

Mi niña
se organizó, fortaleció su rebeldía, enfrentando los sistemas
capitalista y patriarcal desde la lucha popular
y la propuesta feminista.
Gracias al feminismo regresó la mitad de su vida,
ella resiste a la violencia por ser mujer,
a la represión de finales de los setentas, de los ochentas
y al golpe de estado del 2009,
el gas pimienta
y las bombas lacrimógenas...

A mi niña
inocente
emprendedora
ingeniosa pero valiente y rebelde
le dedico estas pocas líneas escritas
con mi puño fuerte.

She felt pain at the loss
of her mother,
a very young
and strong woman.
She was fifty-five years old.
She never could tell her
that she (the mother) had abused her
with so many sorrows
but she understood her
and loved her.
To pronounce the word "love"
was embarrassing
only for her,
her mother.

My girl
of necessity became an adult
and courageously faced
acts of violence
perpetrated by her older brother,
managing to free herself
and her younger sisters.

My girl
got organized, fortified her rebelliousness, defying
capitalist and patriarchal systems through the people's fight
and the feminist movement.
Thanks to feminism she recovered half of her life,
resists gender violence against women,
repression at the end of the Seventies, the Eighties,
and the coup d'état of 2009,
the pepper spray
and teargas bombs...

To my girl
innocent
industrious
resourceful but courageous and rebellious,
I dedicate these few lines written
with my strong fist.

*[Translation by Maria Esperanza Vargas]*

## ALFA REYES

(NO PHOTOGRAPH AVAILABLE)

### Sueño para nuestras comunidades*

Yo sueño que no se pierde la cultura de la comunidad, así
                                                    como la unidad.
Sueño con playas limpias y grandes, con coco.
Sueño que la lluvia cae en un día de vida
que las guerras por los terrenos paran
y cada garífuna piense en el mañana de sus hijos
que cada madre le enseñe a sus hijos ser guerreros.
Sueño que en cada casa abunda la paz y la unidad
que ayudarán a cada niño a no perder su niñez ni su juventud.
Sueño con ese amor y esperanza en cada corazón de los garífunas
y en todos los demás.

---

* Source: *El sonar de las Mujeres de la Tierra y el Mar. Voces de mujeres indígenas, garífunas y campesinas de México, Guatemala y Honduras* [The Sound of Women of the Land and Sea. Voices of Indigenous, Garífuna and Campesina Rural Women from Mexico, Guatemala and Honduras] (Chiapas, Mexico: COMPPA, 2013).

## ALFA REYES

Broadcaster for the Garífuna community radio station, Faluma Bimetu (Sweet Coconut), sponsored by the Black Fraternal Organization of Honduras (OFRANEH), a group that defends ancestral land rights and endeavors to strengthen cultural identity among the Garífunas on the northern coast of Honduras. Participant in poetry workshops for radio broadcasters organized by Popular Communicators for Autonomy (COMPPA).

### Dream for Our Communities

I dream that the culture of the community is not lost, or the
                                                                      unity either.
I dream of big, clean beaches with coconuts.
I dream that the rain falls on a day of life
that wars for the land end
and all Garifunas think of their children's tomorrow
that all mothers teach their children to be fighters.
I dream that peace and unity abound in each house
helping all children avoid losing their childhood or youth.
I dream of the love and hope in the hearts of the Garifunas
and of all others.

*[Translation by Candice Cardwell]*

## ISABEL RIVERA

## (NO PHOTOGRAPH, AT THE POET'S REQUEST)

**Cuerda floja**

Estoy en el punto medio de una cuerda floja
un extremo es blanco
el otro es rojo
parada en un punto sin retorno.

Ya lo dijeron los líderes espiritistas
el golpe estaba escrito y firmado
mejor quédese quieto
todo está controlado.

No hable
no diga
no piense
no ve que lo pueden matar.

Silencio
no mira que está tambaleando
recuerde, la poesía no es ideología
si no, no es poesía
*per se* el arte es arte
bien decían
de esto no se come
pero tiemblan
temen a la palabra que es vida
cuando abre sus brazos y resiste.

Inquisidores del siglo XXI
corren con espadas en sus pies
buscando aniquilar las voces
mandan a las llamas a Domínguez
y a otros poetas benditos
que no caen en el olvido
conectados al pulso universal
de los iluminados.

# ISABEL RIVERA

(Pseudonym, in order to protect the poet's identity in the current circumstances).

## Tightrope

I am at the middle of a tightrope
one extreme is white
the other is red
standing at a point of no return.

The spiritualist leaders told us
the coup was written and signed
you should better be quiet
everything is under control.

Don't speak
don't talk
don't think
don't you see you can be killed.

Silence
don't you see you're swaying
remember, poetry is not ideology
if it is, it isn't poetry
*per se* art is art
they correctly said
you can't eat from it
but they tremble
they fear the word that is life
when it opens its arms and resists.

Inquisitors of the XXI century
run with swords on their feet
seeking to annihilate the voices
send Domínguez to the flames
and other blessed poets
who are not forgotten
connected to the universal pulse
of the enlightened.

## El día que mataron a Georgino
*(Dedicado al periodista Jorge Orellana)*

Bajo el arbusto de la impunidad
un golpe a las ideas
una bala disparada por la ambición
no era de goma.

Un golpe al corazón
astillaron la utopía de un país más justo
una familia rota.

En la orilla de una playa atardecida
la esposa, hijos e hijas
familiares, amigos, amigas, colegas
reunidos para verte ascender
a un nuevo amanecer.

Entre lamentos y llantos
hambrientos por la pronta justicia
aquí y ahora
la otra
la eterna llegará
no hay duda
El
que siempre fue
será.

Te fuiste en medio del apocalipsis de la intolerancia
cerraron tus ojos
pero abrieron los de muchos que creímos que esto
no le ocurría a seres de luz
quijotes de la vida
nobles por vocación.

Los pesares muchas veces son infinitos.

## The Day Georgino Was Killed
*(In honor of the journalist Jorge Orellana)*

Under the bush of impunity
a coup blow to ideas
a bullet shot by ambition
that was not made of rubber.

A blow to the heart
they shattered the utopia of a fairer country
a broken family.

At the edge of a sunset beach
wife, sons and daughters
relatives, men and women friends, colleagues
gathered to see you climb
to a new sunrise.

Between mourning and weeping
hungry for prompt justice
here and now
the other
the eternal will arrive
there is no doubt
He
who always was
will be.

You left in the middle of the apocalypse of intolerance
they closed your eyes
but opened those of many of us who believed that this
could not happen to beings of light
quixotic knights of life
nobles by vocation.

Sorrows are often infinite.

**Te conozco**

Te conozco
te amo
me dueles.

Ingenua
temerosa
secuestrada
manos arriba
boca abajo.

Esclava
no sabes leer ni escribir
burlada
prostituida
enferma.

No hay hermanos
ni hermanas
tus amigos no te entienden
tus enemigos
te creen vencida.

Falsos profetas salen a tu encuentro
saqueadores de la fe
exprimidores de esperanza.

Te conozco
te amo
me dueles.
Desnutrida
desforestada
encarcelada
por tus
hijos e hijas
y recién llegados.

Cínicos
desataron el pandemonio

**I Know You**

I know you
I love you
you pain me.

Naïve
fearful
kidnapped
hands up
face down.

Slave woman
you don't know to read or write
mocked
prostituted
sick.

There are no brothers
or sisters
your friends don't understand you
your enemies
believe you defeated.

False prophets come to you
savagers of faith
wrenchers of hope.

I know you
I love you
you pain me.
Undernourished
deforested
incarcerated
by your
sons and daughters
and those newly arrived.

Cynically
they unleashed the pandemonium

sinvergüenzas
piensan solo en su hoy
la impunidad los cobija
como seres predilectos.

El hartazgo vencerá
pueden pasar
meses
años
siglos
no sé hasta cuándo.

Te llamaremos patria verde
patria justa
tierra amada
lavaremos la sangre
y tristeza de los desterrados.

Diremos te conozco
eres mía
soy responsable
del nuevo aire con olor a fe
mezclado con la frescura de las montañas frondosas
ríos limpios
como las manos de los justos
que de ti cuidan.

Te conozco
te amo
me dueles.

shamelessly
they believe only in their today
impunity shelters them
as privileged beings.

Surfeit will arrive
maybe it lasts
months
years
centuries
I don't know until when.

We will call you green homeland
fair homeland
beloved land
we will wash the blood
and sadness of the displaced.

We will say I know you
you are mine
I am responsible
for the new air perfumed with faith
mixed with the freshness of the thick mountains
clean rivers
like the hands of the just
that take care of you.

I know you
I love you
you pain me.


*[Translations by Andrea Gaytán Cuesta]*

## ELA ROSINDA ROBLES MUÑOZ
(La Ceiba, Atlántida, 1956)

### Maestros Combatientes

Hacia la capital se fueron
los maestros combatientes
exigiendo sus derechos
también la constituyente.
Hicieron caminatas
con palos y pancartas
se tomaron carreteras
y gritaban la consigna
¡Este gobierno es pura lata!

A muchos días de resistencia
no nos pueden vencer
somos fuertes y valientes
somos la ciencia y el saber.
En las calles seguiremos
en las calles viviremos
los maestros combatientes
en resistencia estaremos.

## ELA ROSINDA ROBLES MUÑOZ

Studied Educational Information Technology at Francisco Morazán National Pedagogical University (UPNFM). Honored for her meritorious educational work. Like several other women in this anthology, she does not consider herself a writer, but rather a "poet in training" since the coup d'état. Her method and raw material for writing derive from the street and marches of resistance against the coup, as she explains: "Every time we took to the streets [after June 28, 2009], depending on what was happening that day, I wrote, and ultimately participated by reciting the poems; I never missed a march and have gone through many pairs of shoes since then." Her work is unpublished, but she has been heard on the radio: "I have a poem titled 'Not Forgetting or Pardoning.' Journalist Félix Molina interviewed me and broadcast it on Radio Globo."

### Combatant Teachers

Toward the capital went
the combatant teachers
demanding their rights
and the constitutional assembly.
They marched
with sticks and posters
they took over highways
and yelled the slogan
This government is pure trash!

After many days of resistance
they cannot defeat us
we are strong and brave
we are science and knowledge.
In the streets we will continue
in the streets we will live
the combatant teachers
in resistance we will be.

**Audaces Periodistas**

Sus voces no se callan,
A pesar de la represión.
David Romero y Rony Martínez
Son audaces periodistas
Que informan con pasión.

Los escucha todo el mundo
Por las ondas más sonoras
De radio globo y la televisión.

A las balas no le temen
Ni se venden por un millón
Son periodistas valientes
Orgullo de mi nación.

**Daring Journalists**

Their voices are not silent,
Despite the repression.
David Romero and Rony Martinez
Are daring journalists
Who inform with passion.

The whole world listens to them
Over the loudest waves
Of Radio Globo and television.

They are not afraid of bullets
And won't sell out for a million
They are brave journalists
The pride of my nation.

**Xiomara llegó**

Xiomara se acercaba
el pueblo la saludaba
se oían gritos, canciones,
y la población emocionada.
La caravana era enorme
las calles abarrotadas
hombres, mujeres y niños
con su candidata estaban.
Los golpistas asustados
desde las ventanas miraban
¡Vamos pueblo, vamos pueblo!
Xiomara les gritaba.
A los golpistas les preocupa
la popularidad de Xiomara
se ponen nerviosos
y se ahogan en la nada.

## Xiomara Arrived*

Xiomara came over
the people greeted her
screams, songs were heard
and the crowd, excited.
The caravan was enormous
the streets packed
men, women, and children
standing with their candidate.
The frightened *golpistas*
from the window were watching
Let's go, people! Let's go, people!
Xiomara yelled to them.
The popularity of Xiomara
worries the *golpistas*
they get nervous
and drown into nothingness

*[Translations by Andrew Bentley]*

---

\* Xiomara Castro Sarmiento, wife of deposed president Manuel Zelaya Rosales, LIBRE Party president candidate in the 2013 elections.

**ALEYDA ROMERO**
**(Puerto Cortés, Cortés, 1964)**

## USTEDES

Pisotean dignidades
arrebatan sueños.
Golpean
sin recibir respuesta.
Miran caer luceros
impregnados de sangre,
sin sonrojarse,
no tienen compasión
por los que abren el puño
para pedir vida.
Cuántas voces se apagaron
y se escucharon sus gritos.
Cuántos dejaron de ser,
para que ustedes fueran.
Nunca se equivocan,
lo saben todo.
Ya leyeron la biblia,
comulgan el domingo
en misa de seis.

## ALEYDA ROMERO

University degree in Letters from the National Autonomous University (UNAH), Master's in Higher Education, University of Holguín, Cuba. Current president of the UNAH University Board of Directors. Former teacher and director of the UNAH Regional Center in Choluteca. Participant in recitals. First poems published in *Boletín Literario 18-Conejo* (Literary Bulletin 18-Rabbit); publications in print and virtual journals and local newspapers. Book: *Destiempo* (Wrong Time, 2011), poems and short stories. Unpublished books: *De la guerra y más historias* (On War and Other Stories), stories about the civil war in El Salvador; *Tradiciones orales de San Juancito* (Oral Traditions of San Juancito) and *La comprensión lectora en estudiantes universitarios* (Reading Comprehension in University Students).

## YOU PEOPLE

You trample dignities
snatch dreams.
You knock
without getting a response.
You watch bright stars fall
steeped in blood,
without blushing,
you feel no compassion
for those who open their fist
to beg for life.
So many voices were silenced
and their screams heard.
So many ceased to be,
so that you could be.
You're never wrong,
you know it all.
You have read the Bible,
you take communion on Sunday
at the six o'clock mass.

*[Translation by María Roof]*

## SCARLETH I. ROMERO CANTARERO
(Santa Rosa de Copán, Copán, 1984)

**Hundimiento**

    Como un puñal de hielo
que corta en hilos el frío de mis manos.
Como vuelo a ras de suelo
para no chocar a causa de tanta neblina.
Con pies descalzos, llenos de lodo
dedos entumecidos a causa del frío.
Con las piernas desnudas y el vientre helado
por caminar de frente y sin ruido
ante la indiferencia y frialdad de tus calles.
Con los pechos helados como brújulas nocturnas
que prefieren ser cortados antes de volverse insensibles.
Con la mente divagada, adormecida y bloqueada...
así me quedo ante la sensación de ese témpano de hielo
que cae sobre la cabeza,
la mía que también es tuya.
Así me duelen estas honduras
con nombre de mujer y
cuerpo de centauro.

## SCARLETH I. ROMERO CANTARERO

Studied at Francisco Morazán National Pedagogical University (UPNFM) and the National Autonomous University (UNAH). Active militant and general secretary of the New Democracy Youth (JND), a political organization under the National Coordination of the New Democracy Movement (MND); first national coordinator of the National Youths in Resistance Front (FNJR), and currently a member of their National Coordination. Liberty and Refounding Party (LIBRE) candidate for Congress in 2013.

### Caving In

      Like an ice dagger
that cuts in threads the coldness of my hands.
Like a flight at ground level
to not crash from so much fog.
With bare feet, full of mud
toes numb from the cold.
With bare legs and a frozen belly
from walking straight ahead, noiselessly
amid the indifference and coldness of your streets.
With breasts frozen like night compasses
that prefer to be cut than turn insensitive.
With mind digressed, sleepy, and blocked...
this is how I am facing the sensation of that icicle
that falls over my head,
mine that is also yours.
This is how these depths pain me
with the name of a woman and
body of a centaur.

*[Translation by Andrew Bentley]*

# SARA SALAZAR MELENDEZ
(La Ceiba, Atlántida, 1946)

**El golpe de estado**

Tiranosaurio
estás
vivito y coleando
en Honduras
tránsito obligado del mamut
encuentro
de los trópicos
tierra de nadie
aquí
el pleistoceno
se quedó a dormir
el garrote troglodita
descargó
su golpe artero
rosas de sangre hoy
deshojan pétalos
sobre estas calles
de cal y canto
pobladas de ecos fantasmales
golpe a golpe
palmo a palmo
aquí
existe un estado de golpes

# SARA SALAZAR MELENDEZ

Childhood in San Salvador with her maternal grandparents. Studies in Education in Guatemala. Studies in Medicine upon her return to Honduras, abandoned when she married and dedicated herself to her growing family. Graduated in Law, National Autonomous University (UNAH). Studied Communication in Colombia, 1979, and later taught in the Department of Letters, UNAH, until retirement. Several unpublished poetry collections, among them: *Diente de lobo* (Wolf's Tooth) and *Las preguntas que olvidó Neruda e Izchel* (Questions that Neruda and Izchel Forgot). Her name and engaged poetry are recognized in intellectual circles in Honduras.

## Coup d'État

Tyrannosaurus
you are
alive and kicking
in Honduras
the mammoth's obligatory path
encounter
in the tropics
a no man's land
here
the Pleistocene
stayed overnight
the troglodyte's club
unleashed
its cunning blow
bloody roses today
lose their petals
along these streets
densely
populated by ghostly echoes
blow by blow
step by step
here
exists a state of blows.*

---

* A play on the term in Spanish for coup d'état, "golpe de estado," literally, a strike or blow against the State, here changed to a "state of coups" or "state of blows."

**Hondureñas**

Mujeres
de leche y miel
bañadas
en polen blanco
tierras de pan llevar
orquídeas maceradas
con el golpe de
golpes sin fin
desangradas por
dráculas nativos y extraños
en su carnaval de
inteligent-cia
siglo veintiuno
que hoy anidan
en la barbarie
de Honduras

## Honduran Women

Women
of milk and honey
bathed
in white pollen
fertile lands for corn
orchids crushed
by the blow of
blows without end
bled by
native and foreign Draculas
in their carnival of
twenty-first century
intelligent-cia
who nest today
in the barbarity
of Honduras

**Hoy más que nunca**

Pienso
en ti...
pueblo
te
miro
en ese cactus
surgiendo
de la nada
sin suelo
sin agua
sin tierra
defendiéndote de oscuros designios
resistiendo a
los golpes
pienso
en ti ...
pueblo
Gandhi espinoso
despojo del viento
rehén del desierto
resistiendo
siempre verde
siempre vivo
hoy
más que nunca.

**Today More than Ever**

I am thinking
of you...
the people
I
see you
in that cactus
emerging
out of nothing
without soil
without water
without land
defending yourself from dark intentions
resisting
blows
I am thinking
of you ...
the people
prickly Gandhi
discard of the wind
hostage of the desert
resisting
always green
always alive
today
more than ever.


*[Translations by Candice Cardwell]*

## JÉSSICA SÁNCHEZ (JÉSSICA ISLA)
### (Lima, Peru, 1974)

**Puntos cardinales**

Tengo una seria imposibilidad de levantar mi vista
hacia el norte

Me abruma,
me entristece,
me aprisiona.

Descubro que no puedo con tanta muerte
latiéndome aún entre las venas

No con tanta Centroamérica encima

No con tanta América Latina en las sienes

Para mí,
que desde pequeña he tenido problemas de lateralidad

Y por ende de ubicación,
el sol puede salir por cualquier lado
en cualquier dirección.

## JÉSSICA SÁNCHEZ (JÉSSICA ISLA)

Born in Lima, Peru, dual Honduran and Peruvian nationality. Writer, researcher, feminist activist. Consultant on gender and development. Degree in Letters, National Autonomous University of Honduras (UNAH); Diploma in Public Policy and Gender, FLACSO, Argentina; Master's in Human Development and Gender Studies, Rafael Landívar University, Guatemala. Coordinator, Capiro publishing house, 2000-2004. Founding member, Red Latinoamericana de Escritoras y Artistas Feministas (Latin American Network of Feminist Writers and Artists), 2002. Participant in literary events and congresses in Central America, Mexico, Cuba, and the Dominican Republic. Poems published in anthologies and literary journals. Books: *Antología de narradoras hondureñas* (Anthology of Honduran Women Fiction Writers, 2005); *Infinito cercano* (Close Infinity, 2010).

### Cardinal Points

I have a serious inability to lift my eyes
to the north

It overwhelms me,
it saddens me,
it imprisons me.

I discover I cannot deal with so much death
Still pulsing through my veins

Not as I carry so much Central America with me

Not with so much Latin America at my temples

For me,
who have had problems with laterality since childhood

And hence of location,
the sun can rise on any side
in any direction.

No es posible, me dicen...

Recurro entonces a la prístina memoria
esa que no me falla

Y mis ojos se llenan de mar, de arena,
sal antigua y Caribe

Descubro que mi corazón
no puede saber el norte
porque tiene una
irredenta...

profunda
y
rabiosa miopía

que me aferra implacable
hacia el centro

It is not possible, they tell me...

I turn then to pristine memory
which does not fail me

And my eyes fill up with sea, with sand,
ancient Caribbean salt

I discover that my heart
cannot find north
because it has an
irreparable...

profound
and
raging myopia

that links me relentlessly
to the center

**Rojo**

Mi cuerpo está teñido de rojo.

Rojo de sangre que me devuelven las aceras
de los charcos que solo pueden reflejar
la ignominia y
el dolor.

Las venas se abren, cortadas por miles de navajas invisibles
que se abren paso entre la gente
esa gente que no existe, que es apenas una cifra,
un pálido recuento de la nada.

Las calles, descarnadas se niegan a dar paso a la creencia
de un mundo diferente
porque no puede ser posible vivir
sin pagar la cuota de miseria que a cada quien
le toca.

No hay misericordia en este lugar
donde la gente ríe acaso por olvido
o
por rebeldía.

Los minutos se paran.

En este espectáculo del miedo
esta ya no soy yo.

Alguien más ha ocupado mi lugar.

**Red**

My body is dyed red.

Red of blood that sidewalks return to me
from puddles that can only reflect
ignominy and
pain.

Veins open up, slashed by thousands of invisible knives
that make their way among the people
people who do not exist, who are merely a number,
a pale inventory of nothingness.

The streets, emaciated, refuse to give way to belief
in a different world
because it cannot be possible to live
without paying the share of misery that each one
owes.

There is no mercy in this place
where people laugh perhaps out of forgetfulness
or
rebelliousness.

Minutes stand still.

In this spectacle of fear
I am already not myself.

Someone else has taken my place.

## PRESENTACIÓN
*(A Suyapa, quien inspiró este poema)*

Soy este cuerpo dibujado a golpes
que camina día tras día bajo el sol,
bajo este cielo incierto de máquinas aladas,
en medio de ráfagas de humo y
el sonido de fusiles.
Soy infinidad de rostros:
el de un chico asesinado,
el de la abuela que camina
el de la gente lenca armada de una paciencia infinita
el de la pintora de mantas,
el de la chica de las muletas
que se enfrentan de a pedazos o en conjunto
a las murallas verde olivo cargadas de violencia

Puedo decir que de mi cuerpo salen muchos olores
el de la montuca fresca
el de la tortilla y los frijoles
el de manos sudadas y cuerpos cansados,
pero también
el olor de sangre derramada
el de gas y pólvora
el olor a muerte y a miedo.

Mi garganta
está poblada de voces:
estoy en las discusiones acaloradas de las asambleas
en el grito de la maestra
en el relato de la joven violada,
en la protesta de los golpeados, de las torturadas
en la voz que canta en las calles

Soy miles de sombreros y
cientos de palabras,
soy abrazos, lágrimas,
ternura, carcajadas.
Estoy llena de
sonrisas que iluminan el día

**PRESENTATION**
*To Suyapa, who inspired this poem*

I am this body drawn by blows
that walks day after day under the sun,
under this uncertain sky of winged machines,
amid blasts of smoke and
the sound of rifles.
I am countless faces:
of a murdered boy,
of the marching grandmother
of the Lenca people armed with an infinite patience
of the painter of banners,
of the girl with crutches
who confront in groups or all together
olive green walls charged with violence

I can say many smells leave my body
of fresh montuca
of tortilla and beans
of sweaty hands and weary bodies,
but also
the smell of blood shed
of gas and gun powder
the smell of death and fear.

My throat
is populated with voices:
I am in the heated discussions of the assemblies
in the shout of the teacher
in the story of the young girl raped,
in the protest of the beaten, of the women tortured
in the voice that sings in the streets

I am thousands of hats and
hundreds of words,
I am hugs, tears,
tenderness, laughter.
I am full of
smiles that illuminate the day

colores que vienen de todas partes
tengo alegría, ganas de bailar,
tengo esperanza.

Porque sin mí las calles
se quedarían solas,
porque sin mí las paredes no dirían nada
porque soy tus manos, tus pies cansados,
tu voz.
        Yo soy la resistencia.
*Agosto 2009*

colors that come from everywhere
I have happiness, the desire to dance,
I have hope.

Because without me the streets
would remain empty,
because without me the walls would say nothing
because I am your hands, your weary feet,
your voice.
      I am the resistance.
      *August 2009*


*[Translations by Clarissa J. Williams]*

# CLAUDIA SÁNCHEZ CÁRCAMO
(Tegucigalpa, 1983)

**Valentía**
*Elegía a Erick Fernando Martínez Ávila*

Tegucigalpa
Tan envilecida te encuentro
Que logro ver mi sombra
Reflejada en ti,
En pleno medio día.

Tegucigalpa tan mía,
Tan odiada, tan jodida.

Tegucigalpa
Tengo que ir a un velorio en ti,
Y no es que quiera o deba
Es un sino
Al que no he tenido más opción,
Entre aguacates podridos
Y triadas dieciseisavas.
Tegucigalpa. Hoy quiero coger
Su verde y azul mundo
Y estrellarlo en sí,
Sobre sus cabezas
Echas rabia.

## CLAUDIA SÁNCHEZ CÁRCAMO

Poet and cultural promoter. Degree in Psychology and diplomas in Higher Education and Cultural Promotion, National Autonomous University of Honduras (UNAH). Member of the literary group Máscara suelta (Loose Mask), the National Association of Honduran Women Writers (ANDEH), and Artists in Resistance. Founding member of the Broad Front of Workers in Culture and Arts (FATCA). Poems selected for publication in the anthology, *Caballo verde* (Green Horse, 2006), and in *Ístmica, Revista de la Facultad de Filosofía y Letras* of the National Autonomous University of Costa Rica (2010).

### Courage
*Elegy for Erick Fernando Martínez Ávila*

Tegucigalpa
So prostituted I find you
That I manage to see my shadow
Reflected in you,
At midday.

Tegucigalpa, so mine,
So hated, so messed up.

Tegucigalpa
I have to attend a wake in you,
And it isn't that I want to or must
It's destiny
About which I've had no other choice,
Between rotten avocados
And 3-16 death squads.
Tegucigalpa. Today I want to grab
Their green and blue world
And smash it against them
You sling rage
Upon their heads.

¡Pucha compa!
Que hijos de sus grandísimos
Y putos padres que los engendraron.

Si, ya sabes esos cabrones
Durmiéndote
Entre odios diversos
Y tu necia guerrilla de calle.

Según ellos te llevaron
¿Pero porque, si no te fuiste?
Por lo menos no te vas de mí,
Si logro cada día
Ver esos chicos ojos brillar.

¡Es que puta compa!
Acuérdese de brillar
En mis noches,
Con esa lluvia de risas.

Tegucigalpa. Que gran diferencia
Se crea, entre morir en tus calles
Y el que te maten en una carretera.

Hasta luego compa, amigo, hermano
Hasta siempre Valentina.

Damn it, dude!
What sons of...
And the bastard fathers that engendered them.

Yes, you know those rotten pigs
Putting you to sleep
Between diverse hatreds
And your foolish urban guerrilla.

According to them, they took you
But, why, if you never left?
At least, you don't part from me
If I can manage to see
Those tiny eyes shine every day.

Is just that, dammit, man!
Remember to shine
In my nights
With that rain of laughter.

Tegucigalpa. What great difference
Is created between dying on your streets
And getting killed on a highway.

So long, buddy, friend, brother
Until forever, Valentina.

## Raspando ideas
*Herejía a Walter Tróchez*

El día de su cumpleaños, todos llegaron a su casa; si es suya, ya que ella paga puntualmente el alquiler, pero ninguno fue a saludarla, sino a recordar la cámara que ya no enfocará más ideas, evocando con timorata languidez.

Las veces que a él se le olvido cargar las baterías, vaciar la memoria o mover la tapa del lente; pasando con chillonas risas por todas las veces que él les hiciera la segunda en un trabajo, o las veces que a él le sirvieron de tapadera para evitar que algún cornudo no le mandara cortésmente al averno con el boleto de ida sin retorno.

Además de otras cosas que no volverán a verle hacer, ni encender más velas en su pastel solo por practicar lo que predicaba, sin creer en la inconveniencia de las tarántulas.

**Scraping Ideas**
    *Heresy for Walter Tróchez*

    On his birthday, all of them appeared at her house; yes, it's hers since she pays, punctually, the rent, but none of them came to say hello; instead, they came to remember the useless camera unable to focus on ideas anymore, evoking with timid languor.

    The many times that he forgot to charge the batteries, erase the memory, or remove the lens cap; with strident laughter remembering all the times that he backed them up on a job, or the times that they covered for him to escape from a deceived husband determined to dispatch him courteously with a one-way ticket to hell.

    In addition to other things that they never will see him do again, light more candles on his cake if only to practice what he preached, in total disbelief about the inconvenience of tarantulas.

## Con que agonía pides que...
*A mi Divino amor*

Temiendo que el viento
además de los aguacates
también se lleve mi memoria,
con esa tu idea que es ilógico
no aprender intuiciones sociales
con tu estación conciencia.

Temes no tenerme, ni mantenerme
con tu resistencia tolerando los embates,
de bosquejos abstractos de sub-realidades
de subsistencias inherentes al coraje,
de enemigos que marcan el sendero.

Por qué
¿Los muertos solo salen de nuestros vientres rojos?
¡Es por trabajo de verdes domingos!
Recién lustrados.

Nosotras que esperando no a Godot,
si no que sean miércoles
y regresen al cumplir su plazo.
¿Sabías que no solo se lucha con la caña?
También se hace con el gorgoreo,
desvaneciendo añejos errores
que albergaban encadenadas
plumas de águila.

Escucha, te admiro por ser mujer
que no se queda bajo la luz,
mirando una carreta de arrugadas sombras
sino que buscas salir, y cerrar la puerta
saldando atrás de ti tus cuentas.

Coordina la juventud, lo que conviene a su alma
no es lo que comprende su juicio,
comparte tus ideas, estratega cual ajedrez
y recuerda que el arte lo sentirás en las húmedas alas
que suben en el vaivén salpicado de tu boca.

## With What Agony You Request That...
*To my Divine love*

Afraid that the wind,
in addition to the avocados,
will also take my memory,
with your idea that it is illogical
not to learn social intuitions
with your conscious state.

You're afraid of not having me, of not keeping me
with your resistance enduring the batterings
of abstract sketches of sub-realities,
of acts of subsistence inherent to courage,
of enemies who mark the path.

Why
do the dead emerge only from our red wombs?
It's because of the work of green Sundays
recently shined!

We women waiting, not for Godot
but for it to be Wednesday
and for them to return after their time is up.
Did you know the fight is waged not just with the cane?
It's also fought with the broken song in your throat,
erasing old mistakes
that housed chained
eagle feathers.

Listen, I admire you for being a woman
who doesn't stay stuck under the light,
observing a cart of wrinkled shadows
instead, you try to find a way out and close the door
leaving behind all accounts settled.

Coordinate the youth, what benefits their soul
is not what's understood by their reason,
share your ideas, strategize like a chess player
and remember that you will feel art in the moist wings
that rise in the spattered vibration of your mouth.

Es ya imprescindible en barrios creativos
cansados de matanzas selectivas,
se decidan a conducir una nación
que no cree más en la muerte,
de América combativa.

It's now essential in creative neighborhoods,
tired of selective massacres,
to decide to lead a nation
that no longer believes in the death
of combative America.

*[Translations by María Esperanza Vargas]*

# CLAUDIA SOSA ELVIR
(Tegucigalpa, 1994)

**Arañas y flores**

Soñé con arañas
y agujeros en el mar
Soñé que las serpientes volaban
y las aves se arrastraban.
Soñé con flores disecadas
y la muerte del amado
con niños que gritaban
y asesinos que gozaban.
Abrí los ojos
vi que todo estaba inerte
entonces supe ...

Soñé con mi país.

**CLAUDIA SOSA ELVIR**

Medical student at the National Autonomous University (UNAH). She published some of her poems at thirteen years of age in a bilingual newspaper in the U.S.: "La chica lleva/ The Girl Wears," "Tengo frío/I´m Cold," "El niño corre/ The Boy Runs," "De vez en cuando/ Every Once in a While," "Amigo que cruzas la frontera/Friend Who Crosses the Border," "Volando alto/Flying High," "Inconforme/Dissenting," "El fin del mundo/The End of the World."

**Spiders and Flowers**

I dreamt of spiders
and holes in the sea
I dreamt snakes were flying
and birds were slithering.
I dreamt of dried flowers
and the death of a loved one
of children screaming
and murderers enjoying it.
I opened my eyes
I saw everything was still
then I knew...

I had dreamt of my country.

**Besos y Cuchillos**
*(A las personas que han perdido seres queridos
y, de alguna manera, también a Plutón)*

Quiero pescar sueños apagados
y convertirlos en llamas de amor.
Quiero poder sentarme en la Luna
y brincar hasta Plutón.
Quiero contar las estrellas
y los peces en el mar.
Quiero convertir los cuchillos
en besos, las pistolas en flores
los cañones en relámpagos musicales.
Quiero que las balas sean
flechas de Cupido
y la sangre, libros de revolución.
Quiero sostener tus manos, bailar tango
y conquistar el escenario.
Quiero que el teléfono deje de sonar
que el correo se retrase
ocultarme de la verdad.
Quiero que el beso de la Muerte sea
como los tuyos,
que se haga mi amiga,
que me tome de la mano
y me lleve hacia vos.

**Kisses and Knives**
*(To people who have lost loved ones
and, in a way, also to Pluto)*

I want to catch extinguished dreams
and turn them into flames of love.
I want to be able to sit on the Moon
and jump to Pluto.
I want to count the stars
and the fish in the sea.
I want to transform knives
into kisses, guns into flowers
cannons into musical lightning claps.
I want bullets to be
Cupid's arrows
and blood, revolutionary books.
I want to hold your hands, dance tango
and conquer the stage.
I want the phone to stop ringing
the mail to be delayed
hide myself from the truth.
I want the kiss of Death to be
like yours,
for her to become my friend,
to grasp my hand
and take me to you.


*[Translations by Clarissa J. Williams]*

## SARA TOMÉ
(Tegucigalpa, 1985)

**Resistencia**

Honduras, resiste que el águila habite tus tierras
Resiste a que las barras encarcelen tus sueños
Resiste a cortar las raíces del árbol que da sombra
y alimenta a tus guerreras.
*2012*

## SARA TOMÉ

Feminist, lawyer, graduate of the National Autonomous University (UNAH). Works with the Women's Studies Center-Honduras (CEM-H).

### Resistance

Honduras, resist that the eagle occupy your lands
Resist that bars imprison your dreams
Resist the cutting of the roots whose tree gives shade
and nurtures your women warriors.
    *2012*

*[Translation by Frances Jaeger]*

**CAROLINA TORRES**
**(Tegucigalpa, 1989)**

¿Qué se hace?

> "Esto es lo que tenemos que hacer, nos guste o no.
> Pero ya no tendremos que hacerlo cuando, de nuevo,
> la vida merezca ser vivida...."
> –George Orwell (1984)

Cuando un soñador cae
cuando las calles de un país
están llenas de sangre y sueños.

Cuando vivir y luchar
es el peor delito
cuando la libertad es un pecado.

Cuando las manos se unen
y se fijan horizontes felices
más allá de sus cadenas.

Cuando morir depende
de los dinosaurios retrógrados
y las balas están a su alcance.

Cuando un despierto soñador
es obligado a dormir
y dejar de soñar.

## CAROLINA TORRES

Medical student, National Autonomous University (UNAH). National Secretary of Political and Ideological Training for the Political Organization Los Necios-Honduras (OPLN). Militant in the National Popular Resistance Front (FNRP), the Liberty and Refounding Party (LIBRE) and the Las Necias/Women Fools Marxist Feminist Collective (Colectivo Marxista Las Necias). Member of the Women of Today Poetry Movement (Movimiento poético Las de hoy).

### What To Do?

> *"...This is what we have got to do, unflinchingly. But this is not what we shall be doing when life is worth living again."*
> —George Orwell *(Nineteen Eighty-four)*

When a dreamer falls
when the streets of a country
are full of blood and dreams.

When living and fighting
is the worst offense
when freedom is a sin.

When hands are joined
and happy horizons are fixed
beyond the chains.

When dying depends
on retrograde dinosaurs
and the bullets at their disposal.

When an alert dreamer
is forced to sleep
and stop dreaming.

Cuando cada muerte
nos ensangrienta
los recuerdos
y nos gotea roja
la memoria.

Cuando amar es condenado
y vivir con nuestra propia moral
les enfurece.

Cuando nos morimos
con cada pérdida
lentamente
poco a poco.

¡Cuando decimos basta!
y actuamos para que sea cierto
nos odian por ello
por no callar
porque la sumisión no la conocemos.

¡Cuando llorar deja de ser suficiente!

When every death
sullies our memories
with blood
and our memory
drips red.

When loving is condemned
and living according to our own morals
angers them.

When we all die
with each loss
slowly
little by little.

When we say "Enough!"
and act so that it be true
they hate us for it
because we don't shut up
because we don't know submission

When crying stops being enough!

**El mal no está en las personas, el mal está en el sistema**

*"Que no nos destruya el odio*
*Dignifiquemos la humanidad*
*Hagamos justicia."*

Un grito derrumba la farsa
Otro cementerio clandestino
Donde quienes no pueden llamarse muertos
Mutaron a esperanza:
González, Villalta, Montes
Linares, Castro, Pérez
Velásquez, López, Díaz
Villalobos, Canales, Izaguirre
Martínez, Murillo, Ávila
Muñoz, Vallejo, Figueroa
Avelar, Benítez, Sánchez
Tróchez, Carney, Chávez
Reyes, Gómez, Cano
Recinos, Valle, Alvarenga
Rivera, Andrade, Ortiz
Escoto, López, Betancourt
García, Castillo, Guardado
Colleman, Mondragón, Vindel
Wainwright, Zelaya, Nativí, Becerra
No ajustan las letras
Para tanta sangre derramada
Luchamos
Para reivindicarlos
Solo será cumpliendo el sueño
Que costó sus vidas
Que no morirán jamás
Tenemos sus nombres
Y los de sus asesinos
Aunque no estén
los sabemos todos
Facussé, Flores, Lippman,
Clinton, Bush, Obama
Ferrari, Canahuati, Atala
Reagan, Nixon, Kennedy

## There Are No Bad People, There Is Only a Bad System

*"Let not hate destroy us*
*Let us dignify humanity*
*Let us create justice."*

A cry topples the farce
Another clandestine cemetery
Where those who cannot call themselves dead
Changed into hope:
González, Villalta, Montes
Linares, Castro, Pérez
Velásquez, López, Díaz
Villalobos, Canales, Izaguirre
Martínez, Murillo, Ávila
Muñoz, Vallejo, Figueroa
Avelar, Benítez, Sánchez
Tróchez, Carney, Chávez
Reyes, Gómez, Cano
Recinos, Valle, Alvarenga
Rivera, Andrade, Ortiz
Escoto, López, Betancourt
García, Castillo, Guardado
Colleman, Mondragón, Vindel
Wainwright, Zelaya, Nativí, Becerra
Letters are too few
for so much spilt blood
We fight
To vindicate them
Only by realizing the dream
That cost them their lives
Will they never die
We have their names
And their assassins' names
Even when they are not here
We know who they all are
Facussé, Flores, Lippman,
Clinton, Bush, Obama
Ferrari, Canahuati, Atala
Reagan, Nixon, Kennedy

Lamas, Násser, Kattán
Y pesa la memoria
De nombrar inhumanos
Entonces se repite
En mi cabeza
El mal no está en las personas
El mal está en los sistemas...
El mal no está en las personas
El mal está en los sistemas...
No luchamos sino contra el sistema
El mal no está en las personas
El mal está en los sistemas...
El mal no está en las personas
El mal está en los sistemas...
Cuánta razón y cuán difícil es
El mal no está en las personas
El mal está en los sistemas...
El mal no está en las personas
El mal está en los sistemas.

Lamas, Násser, Kattán
And the inhuman names
Weigh on our memory
Then I repeat
in my head
There are no bad people
There is only a bad system...
There are no bad people
There is only a bad system...
We fight only against the system
There are no bad people
There is only a bad system...
There are no bad people
There is only a bad system...
How right and how difficult it is
There are no bad people
There is only a bad system...
There are no bad people
There is only a bad system.

**10:50 varios días**

Vivo en un país
donde la gente no sólo
no aprendió a volar
simplemente
no saben caminar
están quietos
inmóviles
vacíos.

No disfrutan
despegar del asfalto
de la ciudad
salir
al patio de madrugada
con los pies descalzos
escuchar a sui generis
fumarse las tristezas
perderse entre estrellas
y pensamientos
enterrar fantasmas
en tumbas
selladas
mirar la luna
e invocar gatos.

Suspirar
ante la necesidad
de perderse
de sí mismos
reconocerse
inertes
y aprender
a construir alas de cartón.

Me vuelvo
inerte,
inmóvil,
vacía,

## 10:50 Several Days

I live in a country
where the people not only
did not learn how to fly
simply
they do not know how to walk
they are quiet
motionless
empty.

They do not enjoy
pulling away from the asphalt
of the city
going out
to the yard at dawn
barefoot
listening to sui generis
smoking away sadness
getting lost in the stars
and thoughts
burying ghosts
in sealed
tombs
looking at the moon
and calling to cats.

Sighing
before the necessity
of losing themselves
to themselves
recognizing themselves as
inert
and learning
to make cardboard wings.

I become
inert,
motionless,
empty,

quieta,
terrestre,
calzada,
incapaz de soñar
con alas de cartón y vuelos al sol.
Me convierto en patriota de mi patria de extranjeros e imbéciles.

Niego la tierra
el asfalto
y me reconstruyo
no voy a quedarme
quieta.
No voy a convertirme
en mis miedos.

still,
earthy,
shod,
incapable of dreams
with cardboard wings and flights to the sun.
I become the patriot of my country possessed by foreigners
                                         and imbeciles.

I deny the earth
the asphalt
and I reconstruct myself
I will not remain
quiet.
I will not become
my fears.

*[Translations by Frances Jaeger]*

# EVELYN Y. TORRES MEJÍA
(Tegucigalpa, 1987)

**Silencio de la noche**

El canto de las sirenas que anuncia muerte a los marinos
Ya no se escucha en la mar
Se escucha en calles
En barrios
En colonias
Que no temen más gritar
En la fría media noche
Que quieren libertad.

Ya el temor está dormido
La lucha se ha encendido
La luna como guía
En el silencio de la noche
Que adopta nuevas voces
Que aclaman libertad.

Ya los grillos y saltamontes
Son coros de la gente
Que vence
Ogros verdes
Piratas azules
Que no tienen
Barcos que navegar.

# EVELYN Y. TORRES MEJÍA

Biology student, the National Autonomous University (UNAH). Militant in the Las Necias/Women Fools Marxist Feminist Collective, (Colectivo Marxista Feminista Las Necias) Political Organization Los Necios-Honduras (OPLN) and the National Popular Resistence Front (FNRP). Member of the Women of Today Poetry Movement (Movimiento Poético Las de hoy).

## Silence of Night

The sirens' song that announced death to sailors
Is no longer heard on the sea
It is heard in the streets
In neighborhoods
In subdivisions
That no longer fear shouting
In the cold midnight
That they want freedom.

Now fear is asleep
The fight has ignited
The moon as a guide
In the silence of night
That takes on new voices
That clamor for freedom.

Now the crickets and grasshoppers
Are choruses for people
Who conquer
Green ogres
Blue pirates
Who have no
Boats to sail.

Son vencidos por
La noche
Animada por estrellas
Que desean realizar
Sueños en calles arropadas
En sábanas de humo
El silencio de la noche
Nunca sonó igual.

They are conquered by
The night encouraged
By stars
That want to realize
Dreams in swaddled streets
In sheets of smoke
The silence of night
Never sounded like this.

**Calles**

Ideas andan
nacen
se construyen
con nuevos rostros
viejos nombres.

Surge la duda
la incertidumbre
el malestar
gritos
lágrimas
dolor
vidas
que ya no están.

Nos queda
la alegría
la esperanza
el futuro
las calles
más vivas
con gente
más real.

**Streets**

Ideas wander
are born
are composed
with new faces
old names.

Doubt surfaces
uncertainty
queasiness
cries
tears
pain
lives
that no longer exist.

We are left with
happiness
hope
the future
streets
more alive
with people
more real.

**Ahora**

Me desgarran las miradas
en estos rostros de papel.
Esos nombres que deambulan en
cada carne humana.

Cada papel.

Cada esperanza
de ser un todo
en un país robado
mutilado
donde el plomo
es más palpable
que el pan.

**Now**

The gaze on those paper faces
tears me apart.
Those names that wander in
every bit of human flesh.

Every sheet of paper.

Every hope
to be complete
in a country robbed
mutilated
where lead
is more palpable
than bread.


*[Translations by Frances Jaeger]*

## KAREN VALLADARES
### (Tegucigalpa, 1984)

**Nave de sueños**

> *¿Era yo la voz muerta...?*
> *–Oliverio Girondo*

    Nave de muerte
son mis sueños
o este cuerpo
que habito a diario
o esta voz
que calla
la sombra rota de los espejos
    Nave de sueño
es la muerte
pájaro que vuela alto y lejos
hasta quebrarnos las alas de vidrio
    Naves de muerte
son estas ciudades
que andan con dolor agudo en los pasos
    Nave de muerte
es la vida
donde vienen a morir
los recuerdos
en la vacía plaza de mis ojos.

## KAREN VALLADARES

Poet, writer, cultural promoter. Studied at the Technological University of Honduras (UTH), San Pedro Sula. Cofounder of literary groups such as Poetas del grado cero (Zero Degree Poets) and Máscara suelta (Loose Mask). Member of the National Association of Honduran Women Writers (ANDEH); codirector of the journal *Metáfora*. Participant in many international poetry festivals in Central and South America. Poems published in Honduran and international anthologies and in other publications. Poetry book: *Ciudad inversa* (Inverted City, 2010).

### Ship of Dreams

> *"Was I the dead voice?"*
> –Oliverio Girondo

    Ship of death
are my dreams
or this body
I inhabit daily
or this voice
that silences
the broken shadow of mirrors
    Ship of dream
is death
bird that flies high and far
until it shatters our glass wings
    Ships of death
are these cities
that walk with a sharp pain in every step
    Ship of death
is life
where memories
come to die
in the empty plaza of my eyes.

**Ciudad inversa**

> "...Nadie sueña al mundo"
> ¬Jorge Luis Borges

La ciudad
es una lámpara
un abanico.
    A veces
es un pájaro,
espejo de la muerte,
polvo de nuestro propio cuerpo.
    Un niño que nos usa como barrilete,
un perro que nos lame las sombras.
    Hombres y mujeres
que avanzan en cualquier sentido.
A veces simplemente no avanzan.
    Es larga,
sin movimiento
sin respiración.
    La ciudad es nada más
restos de basura
que vuelan en un cielo negro
o azul
    o amarillo.

    Esta ciudad
es como un mal verso
"es una silenciosa batalla en el ocaso,
    un latido de guitarra, o una vieja espada".
La ciudad
es un río
cargado de piedras
donde la piedra azota al río.
Esta ciudad,
esta precisa ciudad
es el mundo
que nadie sueña.

**Inverted City**

> "...No one dreams the world"
> —Jorge Luis Borges

      The city
is a lamp
a fan.
      Sometimes
it is a bird,
mirror of death,
dust of our own body.
      A child that uses us like a kite,
a dog that licks our shadows.
      Men and women
advancing any which way.
Sometimes they simply don't advance.
      It's long,
without movement
without respiration.
      The city is nothing more
than garbage remains
floating in a black sky
or a blue one
      or yellow.

      This city
is like a bad verse
"it is a silent battle at dusk,
      the beat of a guitar, or an old sword."
The city
is a river
filled with rocks
where the stone lashes the river.
This city,
this precise city,
is the world
that no one dreams.

**Ciudad mía**
> *A Tegucigalpa*

     Ciudad mía
balbuceo,
lenguaje inexplicable,
jade que nos aplasta
los sueños.
     Ciudad mía
palimpsesto roto
hondura de nostalgia
árbol seco que no crece.
     Araña gigantesca:
ya no andas arando el camino
ya envejeciste, ahora preparamos tu sepelio.

## City of Mine
*For Tegucigalpa*

City of mine,
stammering,
inexplicable language,
jade that crushes
our dreams.
City of mine
broken palimpsest
depth of nostalgia
withered tree not growing.
Gigantic spider:
you're no longer marking the way
you got old, now we're arranging your funeral.


*[Translations by María Esperanza Vargas]*

# DIANA E. VALLEJO
(Tegucigalpa, 1969)

## El pueblo

Parece que los fracasos son parte de nuestro sino.
Los buitres rodean el Congreso mustio y cercenado
asechan a los hijos no natos,
vuelan cerca
se quieren comer su voluntad...

Las calumnias son oraciones sin sentido.
Usan de incienso, gas tóxico
sacrificios de horror.

Las trampas mediáticas
se balancean sobre las cabezas del que articula en voz alta
el sentido común.

Las iglesias del medievo han vuelto
son frías, macabras, más peligrosas,
sicarias a sueldo.

# DIANA E. VALLEJO

Writer, photographer, business manager, and human rights activist. Member of the Casa Tomada literary workshop, National Association of Honduran Women Writers (ANDEH) and Greenpeace. Organizer of the 2000 cultural event, "1st Avenue: A Hurricane of Art in Comayagüela." Work published in journals and national and international anthologies. Author of biographies of three women for the One Thousand Women for the Nobel Peace Prize Project, 2005; video director for Honduras, Lunches for Learning Foundation. Awarded third place, 2005, Language Academy's Latin American literary contests, Minas Gerais, Brazil, for her book of poetry *Días urbanas* (Urban Days); awarded first place, 2007. Poetry residency in Mexico sponsored by National Foundation for Culture and the Arts and the Spanish Agency for International Cooperation and Development, 2011; PEN International fellowship, 2013. Currently residing in Mexico.


## The People

It seems failures are part of our fate.
Vultures encircle an amputated, withered Congress
stalking unborn children
flying nearby
hungering to snatch away their will...

False accusations are senseless speeches.
Poisonous gas is used as incense
atrocious sacrifices.

Media traps
hang over the heads of those who voice aloud
common sense.

The churches of the Middle Ages have returned
cold, macabre, more dangerous
salaried assassins.

A nadie llevan a la hoguera,
pero la sangre la cocinan a punta de rifles,
toletes y de calibres gruesos...

Gritar no quiebra el vidrio
no estalla la razón,
gritar suena a desesperación
a caminos promiscuos, a sandalias sueltas
a besos de cocodrilo puntuales y desechos.

Pero hoy tenemos
la voz cantante
la experiencia de un pueblo humillado.
Nadie volverá a cantar para entretener al amo.
Somos el amo...
*31-3-2011*

No one is burned at the stake,
but blood is boiled at gunpoint,
with clubs and large calibers...

Screaming doesn't break glass
doesn't shatter reason,
screaming smacks of desperation
of desultory paths, of loose sandals
of quick, discarded crocodile kisses.

But today we
run the show
have the experience of a humiliated people.
No one will again sing to entertain the master.
We are the master...
    *3-31-2011*

**No hay insultos... ASESINOS...**

He buscado en las palabras
Las justas para insultarlos
He querido ofenderlos
Desearles la muerte,
Desearles dolor
Y no se puede...

¿Cómo?
Son verdugos
No se ofenden nada son
No se mueren porque están muertos
No padecen porque no sienten.

He querido odiarlos
Y son el odio
He querido entenderlos
Pero son la locura...

Busco tener rencor
Y ellos son sus vástagos.

No, no hay insulto
Su nombre es el más degradante
ASESINOS...
    *25-12-2009*

## There Is No Insult... MURDERERS...

I have searched for
the exact words to insult them
I have wanted to offend them
Wish them dead,
Desire pain for them
It can't be done...

How?
They are executioners
They don't take offense, they are nothing
They don't die because they are dead
They don't suffer because they don't feel.

I have tried to hate them
And they are hatred
I have wanted to understand them
But they are madness...

I yearn to cling to malice
And they are its spawn.

No, there is no insult
Their name is the most degrading
MURDERERS...
      *12-25-2009*

## Emo (desde Huehuetlapallan)*

En Huehuetlapallan
un hijo de Comizahual ha sido asesinado,
la tarde es un hacha en el alma...

Escucho desde el horizonte que los colores
de la barba se han hecho espuma entre la gente,
el comentario se hace mar...
rumor de inequidad.

Pakal detalla la ira de las polibestias,
les prepara la sal ardiente donde se calcinarán.

Tocaron al niño de las masas
y el pueblo toma un veneno de odio
han vaciado su reloj.

En ese viejo lugar del albor
un pájaro rojo alzó el vuelo
despabiló a la muchedumbre
coloca gentilmente una aurora,
a la agria vida.

Hoy las balas
son estrellas de muerte
cruzadas de pavor
signos de crueldad
pereció frente a Kukulcan.

---

* Este poema pertenece al libro inédito *Croquis* y fue escrito durante una beca (FONCA y AECID) de la Residencia para artistas Iberoamericanos y Haití en México.

**Emo (from Huehuetlapallan)**\*

In Huehuetlapallan
a son of Comizahual has been assassinated,
the afternoon is an axe to the soul...

From afar I hear that the beard's colors
turned to foam among the people,
comment becomes a sea...
sound of injustice.

Pakal describes the wrath of the polybeasts,
he prepares the searing salt in which they will burn.

They touched the child of the masses
and the people drink hatred's poison
they have drained their hourglass.

At daybreak's ancient site
a red bird took flight
awakening the crowd
gracefully bestowing dawn,
on bitter life.

Bullets today
are death stars
terror crusades
symbols of cruelty
it perished before Kukulcan.


*[Translations by Lezlie Shackell]*

---

\* This poem is part of the unpublished book *Croquis*, written during a residential scholarship for Iberian-American and Haitian artists in Mexico, provided by the National Foundation for Culture and the Arts (Fondo Nacional para la Cultura y las Artes) and the Spanish Agency for International Cooperation and Development (La Agencia Española de Cooperación Internacional para el Desarrollo).

# ANARELLA VÉLEZ OSEJO
# (Tegucigalpa, 1956)

## Memoria

Imágenes corren por mi mente
como gotas de agua
en un día de aguacero
con prisa,
del vacío al tormento,
a la violencia de la mañana que irrumpe en el tiempo,
vivo estos días desesperados
en que la historia se reescribe en nuestras calles,
y siento
que aquí brilla una luz nueva,
caminantes,
resistentes,
transfiguran la ciudad
los muros susurran su existencia
no toleran el olvido.

# ANARELLA VÉLEZ OSEJO

Doctor of History, essayist and cultural promoter. Member of the literary groups PaisPoesible and La Coperacha. Founding member of the publishing house Librería Paradiso. Author of articles in journals such as *Alcaraván, Galatea, Paradiso, Paraninfo, Imaginaria,* and in periodicals of the National Autonomous University of Honduras (UNAH). Columnist for *Tiempo* newspaper; member of the National Association of Honduran Women Writers (ANDEH) and of Feminists in Resistance. Professor of Women's Studies at UNAH. The poems appearing here are from the book *Todas las voces* (All the Voices), published by Librería Paradiso in September 2013.

## Memory

Images race through my mind
like drops of water
on a day of heavy rains,
quickly,
from emptiness to anguish,
to the violence of the morning that bursts onto time,
I live these desperate days
in which history is rewritten in our streets,
and I sense
here the glimmer of a new light,
marchers
resistant,
transfigure the city
the walls whisper their existence
they do not tolerate oblivion.

**Golpes**

Se juntan
se agregan
los golpes de la historia
nuestra historia, la que no está contada
1924, 1963, 2009
Bonilla
López
Innombrables
Innumerables
demasiados
las perras aúllan al paso de las botas opresoras.

## Coups

The coups in history
fall together
meld
our history, the history that goes untold
1924, 1963, 2009
Bonilla
López
Unmentionable
Innumerable
too many
bitches howl at the footfall of the boots of oppression.

**Las de hoy**

Descifradoras
Masturbadoras
Insumisas
Imprescindibles.

**Women Today**

Decipherers
Masturbators
Rebellious
Indispensable.


*[Translations by Gail Ament]*

# APPENDIX

Inter-American Commission on Human Rights [IACHR], Organization of American States
OEA/Ser.L/V/II/
Doc. 55
30 December 2009
Original: Spanish

## HONDURAS: HUMAN RIGHTS AND THE *COUP D'ÉTAT*

Chapter V – continuation

### G. Women's Rights

514. Article 1 of the Inter-American Convention on the Prevention, Punishment and Eradication of Violence against Women (hereinafter, the "Convention on the Prevention of Violence against Women") defines violence against women as "any act or conduct, based on gender, which causes death or physical, sexual or psychological harm or suffering to women, whether in the public or the private sphere." In its preamble, the Convention acknowledges that violence against women is a manifestation of the historically unequal power relations between women and men [606].

515. The Court, following the line of international jurisprudence, has held that sexual violence is any act of a sexual nature which is committed on a person under circumstances that are coercive. Sexual violence is not limited to physical invasion of the human body and may even include acts that involve no penetration at all or even physical contact [607].

516. The Inter-American Court has also indicated that in the context of internal or international armed conflict the parties often employ sexual violence against women as an instrument of punishment and suppression. The use of official authority to violate the rights of women in an internal armed conflict affects them directly, and can also be intended as retaliation or as a message to society [608].

517. On the issue of women deprived of their liberty, international standards indicate that the rape of detainees by a State agent is a particularly grave and abhorrent crime, in view of the vulnerability and defenselessness of the victim [609]. Rape is a highly traumatic experience that can have severe consequences [610] and causes great physical and psychological harm, leaving the victim feeling "debased and violated both physically and emotionally" and with deep psychological scars that do not heal as quickly as other forms of physical and mental violence [611].

518. The IACHR also received testimony revealing that both in the context of suppression of demonstrations and unlawful detentions, women were subjected to verbal abuse and sexual violence. The Inter-American Court has already held that acts of violence specifically targeted against women are in many cases used as "a symbolic means to humiliate the other party" [612]. The Commission has held repeatedly that the commission of rape by State agents is equivalent to torture.

519. The Commission has learned that members of the security forces reportedly raped women detained after demonstrations. The Commission took testimony from one woman in particular, who after being detained at a demonstration, had allegedly been raped by four soldiers, who had also forced their police batons into her vagina [613].

520. During its 137th regular session, the Commission was informed that at least seven other women had reportedly been raped by security agents in the context of the public demonstrations held to protest against the *coup d'état*. However, they had refrained from filing their complaints for fear of reprisals and mistrust of the system of justice.

521. The Commission also received information to the effect that women were systematically beaten on their buttocks, thighs and on the rear side of their legs [614]. According to the testimony, the police agents touched women in sexual

ways while the women were under arrest; in some cases, police prodded women's genitalia and crotches with their batons [615]. Male officers also involved female officers asking them to "mess" with the detainees [616]. The Commission received the following testimony:

> When they arrest us, they verbally abuse us; they say things like: "Old whores, why aren't you home making dinner? What are you looking for here? Oh, what you want is sex. What you're trying to say is that you want to get it on." They humiliate us. And then there's the physical harm as well. The beatings they administer to women on the buttocks and the legs... and they put their police batons between our legs to intimidate us, and then ask us if we want to have sex [617].

522. The IACHR also received testimony from a woman who was trapped between military roadblocks erected on July 24 on the road from Las Manos to the border. According to her account, she spent three days without food or water and unable to attend to her biological needs. She was so frightened by the entire situation that she suffered a hemorrhage, but the soldiers gave her nothing to take care of her personal hygiene. The entire time she was detained, she was terrified of being raped by the soldiers, given the psychological aggression she had suffered [618].

523. Another woman, detained on July 24 at the departmental police station of the municipality of Danlí, said that they stripped her and ordered her to bend over, which she refused to do. This all happened in the presence of her son, who was 11 years old and reportedly cried the entire time. She also said that after being put into the cells, the women were searched in an obscene fashion; agents touched them, hit the women's genitalia with their batons [619] and then threatened to burn them [620].

524. The Movimiento de Feministas en Resistencia [Feminists Movement in Resistance] has played an active role and has openly expressed its condemnation of the *coup d'état*.

As a result, their members have been mistreated by security forces on various occasions [621]. This organization has repeatedly denounced the violence against women and the failure of CONADEH and the Public Prosecutor's Office to act on the complaints filed at the domestic level [622]. Specifically, the Movimiento de Mujeres por la Paz, "Visitación Padilla" [Visitation Padilla Women's Pro-Peace Movement] stated that it made presentations to the Special Prosecutor for Women to make her aware of the fact that military and police agents were detaining women in the eastern sector of the country, stripping them, raping them and then releasing them without their underwear [623].

525. During a thematic hearing held during the 137th regular session of the IACHR, the representatives of Feminists in Resistance reiterated that the security forces were verbally abusive of women who participate in the demonstrations, calling them "whores," "revolting", "you want us to rape you" or "go home and take care of the kids." They also reported that no complaints on the violation of women's rights have been filed before local authorities because women have no confidence in the justice system, because the authorities tend to ignore these complaints, or because women are frequently expected to file them before the perpetrators themselves.

526. The representatives of Feminists in Resistance also described how surveillance and security operations continue, as do death threats, laden with sexual overtones and directed at female human rights defenders (both face-to-face and by cell phone).

527. There were complaints that women working for institutions charged with promoting and protecting women's rights were being persecuted. It was also said that plans within the National Women's Institute were suspended for lack of budget, as there was no international cooperation. Also, there is a plan to merge that institution with other social programs, thereby rendering women's issues invisible. Coordinators of the municipal women's affairs offices were re-

portedly being persecuted and threatened. The representatives complained that significant ground had been lost in the area of reproductive rights and maternal health care. They also said that the Office of the Special Prosecutor for Women has lost all credibility, that it does not investigate the violations reported and that the guarantees of due process are not observed.

528. The Supreme Court asserted the following in its observations: "The allegation that members of the security forces raped and otherwise sexually molested women detained in demonstrations is flatly denied inasmuch as no such events have been reported to law enforcement officials and the justice system and the allegations themselves are based on conjecture" [624]

529. A recurring theme in the information reported is that law enforcement personnel discriminate against women. They are not only beaten on numerous occasions but are also victims of sexual violence. This situation is compounded by the difficulties filing complaints at the domestic level and securing the prosecution and punishment against the state agents responsible for these acts.

====

References:
[606] IACHR, *Report of the Inter-American Commission on Human Rights on the Status of Women in the Americas*, OEA/Ser.L/V/II.100, Doc. 17, 13 October 1998.
[607] I/A Court H.R., *Miguel Castro Castro Prison vs. Peru Case*. Merits, Reparations and Costs. Judgment of November 25, 2006. Series C No. 160, paragraph 306; International Criminal Tribunal for Rwanda. *Case of Prosecutor vs. Jean-Paul Akayesu,* Judgment of September 2, 1998.
[608] I/A Court H.R., *Castro Castro Prison vs. Peru Case*, op. cit., paragraph 224.
[609] European Court of Human Rights, Case of Aydin v. Turkey, Judgment of September 25, 1997, paragraph 83.
[610] United Nations, Commission on Human Rights. 50th session, Question of the Human Rights of All Persons Subject to Any Form of Detention or Imprisonment, in particu-

lar: torture and other cruel, inhuman or degrading treatment or punishment. Report of the Special Rapporteur, Mr. Nigel S. Rodley, submitted pursuant to the Commission on Human Rights resolution 1992/32. Doc. E/CN.4/1995/34 of January 12, 1995, paragraph 19.

[611] ECHR Case of Aydin v. Turkey, op. cit., paragraph 83; I/A Court H.R., Castro Castro Prison vs. Peru Case, op. cit., paragraph 311.

[612] I/A Court H.R., Castro Castro Prison vs. Peru Case, *op. cit.*, paragraph 223. See also, U.N., Committee for the Elimination of Discrimination against Women, 11th session. General Recommendation 19 "Violence against women." Doc. HRI/GEN/1/Rev. 1 at 84 (1994), paragraph 16; United Nations Commission on Human Rights, 57th session, 2001, Report of the Special Rapporteur on violence against women, its causes and consequences, Ms. Radhika Coomaraswamy, submitted in accordance with the Commission on Human Rights resolution 2000/45, "Violence against women perpetrated and/or condoned by the State during times of armed conflict (1997-2000)", E/CN.4/2001/73, paragraph 44.

[613] Jesuit Ministries' Team of Reflection, Research and Communication in Honduras [Equipo de Reflexión, Investigación y Comunicación de la Compañía de Jesús en Honduras] (ERIC), Preliminary Report. *Violación a los derechos humanos fundamentales* [*Violation of basic human rights*], El Progreso, Department of Yoro, received by the IACHR on August 17, 2009.

[614] *Amnesty International, Honduras: Human rights crisis threatens as repression increases*, e-mail received on September 3, 2009. Testimony of D.X.F.S., taken by the IACHR in Tegucigalpa on August 19, 2009 (No. 14). Testimony of S.C.C.E., taken by the IACHR in Tegucigalpa on August 19, 2009 (No. 111). Testimony of H.S.M.S., taken by the IACHR in Tegucigalpa on August 19, 2009 (No. 206). Testimony of E.Z.A., taken by the IACHR in Tegucigalpa on August 19, 2009 (No. 1).

[615] Testimony of G.G., taken by the IACHR in Tegucigalpa on August 18, 2009 (No. 293).

[616] Testimony of A.V.O., taken by the IACHR in Tegucigalpa on August 21, 2009 (No. 243). Testimony of A.L.O.C.

and J.P.M.A., taken by the IACHR en Tegucigalpa on August 17, 2009 (No. 123).
[617] Testimony of I.M., taken at the meeting of human rights defenders in San Pedro Sula on August 19, 2009.
[618] Testimony of M.U., taken by the IACHR in Tegucigalpa on August 21, 2009 (No. 222). Testimony of N.G.B., taken by the IACHR in Comayagua on August 20, 2009 (No. 87)
[619] Testimony of C.M.R., cited in CIPRODEH, *Reporte de violaciones de derechos humanos en Honduras en el marco del golpe de Estado [Report on human rights violations in Honduras in the context of the coup d'état]*, received by the IACHR in Tegucigalpa on August 17, 2009.
[620] Testimony of T.J.R., cited in CIPRODEH, *Reporte de violaciones [Report on human rights violations]*, op. cit.
[621] Communiqués from the Movimiento de Mujeres por la Paz "Visitación Padilla" ["Visitación Padilla. Women's Pro-Peace Movement]. Information received by the IACHR in Tegucigalpa on August 18, 2009 (No. 49). Testimony of S.M., taken by the IACHR at the meeting of social leaders on August 17, 2009.
[622] Testimony of S.M. Information supplied by the Movement of Feminists in Resistance and received by the IACHR in Tegucigalpa on August 19, 2009 (No. 488).
[623] Information supplied by the Movimiento de Mujeres por la Paz "Visitación Padilla", received by the IACHR in Tegucigalpa on August 18, 2009 (No. 49). On July 4, 2009, this organization was denied permission to broadcast its radio program "AQUÍ ENTRE CHONAS."
[624] Observations made by the State of Honduras to the IACHR's Report, dated December 22, 2009 and signed by the Chief Justice of the Supreme Court, pp. 17-18, paragraph 44.

*Source:*
*http://cidh.org/countryrep/Honduras09eng/Chap.5.a.htm#_ftnref135.*

# BACK COVER COMMENTARY, FIRST EDITON IN SPANISH
## "*Custos, quid de nocte?*"[*]

Rick Mc Callister
Delaware State University

    A long night has descended over Honduras with roaming nocturnal armies formed by every type of pernicious vermin-a superlumpen of the powerful and criminal classes using all the rights and privileges of authority to eliminate anyone who might imperil their reign of theft, murder and drug trafficking.
    Only the guardians of the night, at great personal risk, defy Hun Kamé and the other infernal lords of Xibalbá. They include educators, journalist, lawyers, and union members, as well everyday people who thirst for moral rectitude. They are the happy patriots who struggle for the good of all, the sad patriots who have given their lives. Among these saviors of dignity, we find the daughters of the Creator Goddess Xmukané, women who fight with pen and voice, women with years of struggle against injustice in a nation which, even in the Best of time, has always suffered from machismo and barriers based on social class.
    As guardians, they shine the light of truth upon poisonous insects that act with impunity; they remind us of evil deeds and note that the hours of the night are limited.
    Among them is Lety Elvir, one of the most distinguished poets of Americas, as indefatigable writer whose words, whether honeyed or harsh, always hit the mark.

---

[*] Watchman, what is left of the night? Implied but not cited is the Watchman's reply: "Morning is coming, but also the night." Isaiah 21.11.

## TRANSLATORS

**Gail Ament** is Professor of Spanish at Morningside College, where she teaches courses in advanced composition and conversation and contemporary Latin American literature. She earned her Ph.D. at the University of Washington in 1998, with her doctoral dissertation, "The New Mayan Scribe: Contemporary Indigenous Writers of Guatemala." She fondly remembers the conference of the Congreso Internacional de Literatura Centroamericana (CILCA) that took place in Tegucigalpa in 1994, where the warm welcome and spirited participation of Hondurans from many walks of life turned the conference into an unforgettable cultural happening. Email: ament@morningside.edu.

**Alba F. Aragón** is Assistant Professor of Comparative Literature at Bridgewater State University in Bridgewater, MA. She received her Ph.D. in Romance Languages and Literatures from Harvard University. Her manuscript, "The Rhetoric of Fashion in Latin America," explores fashion's role in the cultural imaginaries of modernity in Latin America since the nineteenth century. Some of her translations of Nicaraguan women's poetry have appeared in Vidaluz Meneses, *Flame in the Air: Bilingual Poetry Edition* (2013), edited by María Roof. Email: Alba.Aragon@bridgew.edu.

**Jonathan F. Arries** is Associate Professor of Modern Languages at the College of William and Mary (Ph.D., University of Wisconsin–Madison). A specialist in Curriculum & Instruction and Foreign Language Education, he teaches a range of courses in Hispanic Studies that include Spanish language, translation, Border Studies, and also TESOL. Jonathan has been a volunteer medical interpreter in Honduras and in Virginia. Whenever possible, he teaches a service-learning course in Nicaragua in which U.S. students teach English in elementary schools in Managua as they research, design and implement projects of interest to that community. Jonathan´s current research looks at methods of teaching and learning in two different contexts: teaching U.S. students to analyze the discourse of propaganda and censorship, and teaching literacy skills (both English and Spanish) to incarcerated adults in the U.S. Email: jfarri@wm.edu.

Jonathan would like to recognize his colleague Regina Root, a model scholar whose commitment to "lo ético y lo estético" is inspiring.

**Andrew Bentley** is a Ph.D. student of Hispanic Cultural Studies at Michigan State University. He holds an M.A. in Spanish Language, Literature, and Culture from Syracuse University and a B.A. in Spanish Language and Literature and Anthropology from the State University of New York at Potsdam. His main area of research is Central America's post-conflict literary and cultural production. He explores how different texts—ethnographic approaches, graffiti, novels, photography, and street performances—represent the roles of masculinity and violence in new urban imaginaries after the Guatemalan Civil War. This is his first project involving Honduras. Email: bentle94@msu.edu.

Andrew sets aside special mention to express his deepest gratitude to colleague Jennifer Monti (Ph.D. student at the University of California, Los Angeles) for her encouragement, feedback, rigorous attention to detail, and constant reminders that academia is a joyous endeavor.

**Candice Cardwell** is a 2014 graduate of Howard University, where she received her B.A. in Spanish. In 2012 she studied Spanish literature in Granada, Spain, at the Universidad de Granada, Centro de Lenguas Modernas. She currently lives in Madrid and works as an English language and cultural assistant for grades 1-6 at a bilingual primary school in the district of Carabanchel. She has traveled to Morocco, Portugal, France, Italy, and England with the hopes of exploring all corners of the world. She plans to return home to New York to pursue her Master's degree for dual certification in general childhood education and special education with a bilingual extension and begin her career as an educator. Email: candicecardwell@gmail.com.

**Linda J. Craft** is Professor of Spanish and Latin American Literature and Culture at North Park University, Chicago (Ph.D., Northwestern University). She has published several books, including *Novels of Testimony and Resistance from Central America* (1997); a translation of Salvadoran Manlio Argueta's novelized memoir, *Siglo de O(g)ro, Once Upon a Time[bomb]* (2007); and a co-edited collection of critical readings of Argueta's work, *Desde la hamaca al trono y al más allá* (From the Hammock to the Throne and Beyond, 2013), in addition to many essays and reviews. She remembers with bemused cynicism a brief conversation she had in 1983 with a U.S. Consular official in Tegucigalpa who predicted that the neighboring "Sandinistas are here to stay." Email: Lcraft@northpark.edu.

**Kathleen Cunniffe** is a Ph.D. student in the Department of Spanish and Portuguese at Temple University in Philadelphia. She holds a B.A. in Spanish and Latin American Studies from Albright College in Reading, PA, and a Master's degree in Latin American Studies from the University of New Mexico. Her current research focuses on Irish connections and intertextualities in contemporary Spanish American literature. Other interests, related to the courses she teaches at Albright College, are female revolutionary narratives, transnational identities as expressed in borderlands and migrant literature, and U.S.-Latin American relations. In addition to her teaching, Kathleen serves on the board of trustees for a bilingual charter school in Gettysburg, PA. She is also an officer for the Middle Atlantic Council of Latin American Studies (MACLAS). Kathy won the MACLAS 2002 Juan Espadas Prize for best undergraduate paper. Email: kcunniffe@hotmail.com.

> Kathleen would like to thank her friends and colleagues, Angel and Gabriela Díaz-Dávalos, for their consultations regarding these translations. She is also grateful to her MACLAS colleague, María Roof, for the opportunity to participate in this project.

**Andrea Adhara Gaytán Cuesta** has a M.A. in International Relations from Università di Bologna, Italy, and a B.A. in International Relations from Universidad Latina de América, Mexico. *Michoacana* and *Jarocha* by adoption, she has worked with international programs in Mexico and at the College of William and Mary. Her main interests involve Migration Studies, particularly, Feminization of International Migrations; Mexican and Latin American Cultural Studies, and cultural productions that derive from social movements, environmental issues, and neo-colonialism. She presented her research at the 2013 meeting of the Middle Atlantic Council of Latin American Studies (MACLAS). She is currently enrolled in the Ph.D. program in Spanish Literature at Rutgers, the State University of New Jersey. Email: andreagaytan@gmail.com.

**Janet N. Gold** is the author of several books and essays on the literature of Central America, including *Clementina Suárez, Her Life and Poetry* and *Culture and Customs of Honduras*. Her most recent work, *Silver Mountain/La montaña plateada*, is a story for young people based on the history of the mining town of Santa Lucía, Honduras. She teaches Latin American literature and culture at the University of New Hampshire. She invites correspondence at: janetngold@gmail.com.

**Frances Jaeger** is Associate Professor of Spanish at Northern Illinois University (Ph.D., University of Illinois at Urbana-Champaign). She has published articles in national and international journals on the works of Roque Dalton, Nicolas Guillén, Rosa María Britton, Gloria Guardia and Miguel Angel Asturias. Her current areas of research include issues of nation, race and gender in the Panamanian Canal Novel. Poetry has always been a particular area of interest since her dissertation on contemporary women Sandinista poets, Gioconda Belli, Vidaluz Meneses, Daisy Zamora and Michèle Najlis. Email: fjaeger@niu.edu.

**Joan F. Marx** is Professor of Spanish and Director of the Spanish Program at Muhlenberg College. She earned her Ph.D. at Rutgers University (1985), writing her doctoral dissertation on "Aztec Imagery and Surrealism in the Narrative Work of Elena Garro: A Thematic Approach." Her professional work in contemporary Latin American literature includes scholarly publications in national and international literary journals as well as presentations of her work at national and international meetings. Her research interests coincide with the courses that she teaches, which include *The Literature of Conquest and Colonization in Spanish America, Postcolonial Realities in Spanish American Literature, Border Literature, Human Rights Literature in the Americas*, and the Capstone Seminar, *Writing the Jewish Diaspora from Spain to the Americas*. She has long been a member of the Middle Atlantic Council of Latin American Studies (MACLAS), and served for many years as the editor of its journal, *Latin American Essays*. Email: marx@muhlenberg.edu.

**Marie Pfaff** is a student at Concordia University, Montreal, Canada, studying Spanish Language and Culture and Anthropology. She was raised in a trilingual environment (French, English, Spanish), studied at the Escuela Argentina and the Bethesda International School and graduated from the Lycée Rochambeau in Maryland. She has lived in France and Africa, traveled to Venezuela, Brazil, Cape Verde and Spain, among other countries, and interned at an international consulting firm. She is planning a career in international culture. Email: marie.pfaff921@gmail.com.

**Christopher Potts** has a B.A. in Spanish from Howard University, where he minored in Arabic studies. During his years at Howard, he spent a semester in the Dominican Republic at the Universidad Autónoma de Santo Domingo and the Instituto Tecnológico de Santo Domingo, where he studied Dominican social realities and culture. His experiences there motivated him to write his senior thesis on the political relationship between the U.S. and the Dominican Republic, "*La Fiesta del Chivo* y las relaciones interamericanas: República Dominicana y Estados Unidos." Email: cjpotts91@gmail.com.

Chris would like to express gratitude to Dr. Maria Roof for the opportunity to contribute to this project.

**María Roof** is Associate Professor Emerita at Howard University, where she taught Latin American literature and cultures, translation, and women studies. She is editor and translator of *Vidaluz Meneses, Flame in the Air: Bilingual Poetry Edition* (2013), which won the 2014 Best Bilingual Poetry Book Prize in the International Latino Book Awards, and was an Honorable Mention finalist for the 2014 Balcones Poetry Prize. She translated Argentine author Graciela Maglia's poetry collection, *Entrópicos/Entropics: Bilingual Edition* (2013). Her translations and analyses of poetry have appeared in numerous publications, including *Revista Iberoamericana, Aportaciones para una historia de la literatura de mujeres de América Central, MACLAS Latin American Essays,* and *The Facts on File Companion to World Poetry, 1900 to the Present*. María and Rick Mc Callister are collaborating on a series of bilingual anthologies of contemporary Central American women poets. María is secretary of the Middle Atlantic Council of Latin American Studies (MACLAS). Email: mroof@howard.edu.

María would like to thank the team of translators who enthusiastically volunteered their talents and expertise for this project. Special appreciation to Regina A. Root, who volunteered her own efforts and suggested other possible translators. Thanks to her, the translations were done in record time. My appreciation also to language consultants Françoise Pfaff, Graciela Maglia, Amelia Mondragón and María del Pilar Polo.

**Regina A. Root** received her Ph.D. in Hispanic Languages and Literatures from the University of California at Berkeley. She has written, edited and co-edited *The Handbook of Fashion Studies* (Bloomsbury, 2013), *Couture and Consensus: Fashion and Politics in Postcolonial Argentina* (University of Minnesota Press, 2010), and *The Latin American Fashion Reader* (Bloomsbury, 2005), among others. She has served as consulting editor of *Encyclopedia of Latin American Women Authors* and translated Gabriel Giovanetti's

*Light From the East: A Photographic Journey Into the Ways of the Muslim Faith* and various essays. She directs Hispanic Studies at the College of William and Mary. Regina is a long-time member of the Middle Atlantic Council of Latin American Studies (MACLAS). She served as MACLAS president in 2009-2010 and twice won its Arthur P. Whitaker Best Book Prize: in 2006 for *The Latin American Fashion Reader* and in 2012 for *Couture and Consensus*. Email: root.regina@gmail.com.

Regina would like to acknowledge the support for her translation work given by her parents, Steven MacAlpine and Heidi MacAlpine.

**Stephanie Saunders** is Assistant Professor of Spanish at Capital University in Columbus, Ohio. Stephanie received her B.A. from Lyon College and her M.A. and Ph.D. in Hispanic Studies from the University of Kentucky. She specializes in gender and body studies in Hispanic literature and popular culture. Stephanie has presented and published internationally on cultural studies and identity. She has served as a Visiting Researcher in Residence at the Pontificia Universidad Católica in Santiago, Chile. She has published several articles on fashion and currently is working on a project involving eco-fashion in Chile. She also is working with an international research team on the economic crisis and migration in Spain. In December 2014 she co-led a service learning group to work with the BriBri indigenous peoples of Costa Rica. Stephanie has presented her research at meetings of the Middle Atlantic Council of Latin American Studies (MACLAS). Email: ssaunde2@capital.edu.

Stephanie would like to thank her colleague and dear friend, María José Delgado, for her consultation regarding these translations. Her keen eye, patience and passion for women's rights are greatly appreciated.

**Lezlie Shackell** received her B.S. in Spanish from Illinois State University, her teaching certification from Northern Illinois University, and her M.A. in Spanish from Howard University. She has presented and published essays on Afro-Ecuadorians, the Armed Forces in Ecuador, and the integration of women into the Armed Forces in Latin America. She has lived in Panama and Ecuador, and currently resides in Asunción, Paraguay, where she is the High School Principal for the bilingual school, Colegio Lumen. Lezlie presented her research at several meetings of the Middle Atlantic Council of Latin American Studies (MACLAS), and won its 2008 John D. Martz III Prize for the best paper presented by a graduate student. Email: lezlieparra@hotmail.com.

**María Esperanza Vargas.** Nicaraguan poet, narrator, and translator. She has a B.A. in English and a B.A. in Philosophy from the University of Alabama at Birmingham (UAB), and an M.A. in Spanish from the University of Alabama (UA). In 2013, she earned her Ph.D. at UA, writing her doctoral dissertation on "Transgression, Transformation, and Paradox in the Autobiography of the Lieutenant Nun." She has been an editor for the magazines *Astarte* and *Poems, Memoirs, Stories...*, and for *Hispania* and *La Tatuana*, a magazine of the University of Alabama. Her poems, stories, and essays have appeared in magazines and in anthologies such as *Mujeres de sol y luna* (Women of Sun and Moon, Managua, 2007), *En las redes de la poesía* (In Poetry's Nets, Managua, 2008), *Poemas escogidos de la poesía nicaragüense actual* (Selected Contemporary Poems from Nicaragua, London, 2008) and *Cuentos nicaragüenses de ayer y hoy* (Nicaraguan Stories of Yesterday and Today, Miami, 2014). In 2009, María won the Hackney Award for her poems in English, and in 2003, the Rafaela Contreras Prize for Central American Women Writers for her book, *Los ojos abiertos del silencio* (The Open Eyes of Silence). Email: mariaembv@gmail.com.

**Mesi Walton** teaches Spanish and is a Ph.D. student in African Studies at Howard University. She holds a B.S. in Human Development, a Master's in Education and M.A. in Spanish Language and Linguistics from Howard. Her research focuses on retentions of African cultural practices in Latin America, especially in dance, music, instruments, language and spirituality. As a cultural consultant Ms. Walton does research presentations, teaches dance and music, performs and has led delegations to Venezuela and Colombia. She founded and directs the Diaspora Dance company, which has performed in cultural exchanges in the U.S., Latin America and the Caribbean. She has presented her research at a meeting of the Middle Atlantic Council of Latin American Studies (MACLAS). Email: mewalton1@yahoo.com.

Mesi is grateful for the opportunity offered by her professor, Dr. Maria Roof, to participate in this work and hopes to meet the authors someday.

**Clarissa J. Williams,** earned her Ph.D. in Communication & Culture and M.A. in Spanish at Howard University in Washington, D.C. Her research interests include Afro-Latino identity (re)negotiation; salsa music as a medium of sociopolitical protest; and most recently, representations of Afro-Brazilian women in Brazilian media. In 2011, she was awarded a grant from the U.S. Department of Education to enroll at the Federal University of Bahia in Salvador da Bahia and conduct research for her dissertation. She immersed herself in Brazilian culture for six months and gained critical insight into social and political issues affecting the working-class population. Clarissa has presented her research at professional venues, including the meeting in Ponce, Puerto Rico, of the Middle Atlantic Council of Latin American Studies (MACLAS). Currently, she shares her experiences with students in Spanish courses at Howard University, Communication courses at the College of Southern Maryland, and Spanish at Prince George's Community College's Veterans Upward Bound Program. Email: Clarissa.williams@live.com.

Printed in the United States of America
for Casasola LLC
MMXV

www.ingramcontent.com/pod-product-compliance
Lightning Source LLC
Chambersburg PA
CBHW070932230426
43666CB00011B/2407